SCHOLASTIC

Your Best Year Yet!
A GUIDE TO
Purposeful Planning & Effective Classroom Organization

SHOSHANA WOLFE

New York • Toronto • London • Auckland • Sydney
Mexico City • New Delhi • Hong Kong • Buenos Aires

Teaching Resources

DEDICATION

For the 2001–2002 staff of P.S. 89, Manhattan,
who never forgot what mattered most.

Scholastic Inc. grants teachers permission to photocopy the designated reproducible pages from this book for classroom use. No other part of this publication may be reproduced in whole or in part, or stored in a retrieval system, or transmitted in any form or by any means, electronic, mechanical, photocopying, recording, or otherwise, without written permission of the publisher. For information regarding permission, write to Scholastic Inc., 557 Broadway, New York, NY 10012.

Cover design by Vitomir Zarkovic
Interior design by Maria Lilja
Interior illustrations by Shoshana Wolfe
Interior photos by Shoshana Wolfe and Tim Waugh

ISBN 0-439-51371-5

Copyright © 2006 by Shoshana Wolfe
All rights reserved. Published by Scholastic Inc.
Printed in the U.S.A.

1 2 3 4 5 6 7 8 9 10   40   12 11 10 09 08 07 06

Contents

Introduction 4

CHAPTER 1: The Foundation of a Classroom That Works:
Creating a Classroom Community in the Upper Grades 8
- The Nuts and Bolts of Building Community 9

CHAPTER 2: Purposeful Planning & Tools for Managing Time 16
- The Challenge for Teachers 17
- The Working Calendar, Backbone of Your Year-Long Plan 20
- Curriculum-Building Resources 31
- Customizing a Planbook: Your Weekly Schedule 45
- The Artifact Binder: A Place for Records and Resources 49
- Summary 52
- Reproducibles 54

CHAPTER 3: Designing a Classroom That Will Stay Organized 62
- Six Principles for Room Design 63
- Five Classrooms, Five Approaches 67
- Create Your Room 75
- Classroom Design Grid 77
- Cleaning Out and Paring Down 78
- Organizing Classroom Materials 80
- Materials Sorting Chart 83
- Making Students Your Allies in Maintaining the Classroom 89
- Summary 93

CHAPTER 4: Taming All That Paper: *Classwork, Homework, Record-Keeping, and Reporting Student Progress* 94
- Preventing Paper Clutter 95
- Managing the Paper You Need 97
- A System That Works 98
- The System in Action 104
- The Homework Factor 107
- Truly Useful Assessment 112
- Record-Keeping and Reporting Student Progress 117
- Guidelines for Conducting Successful Parent Conferences 119
- Summary 123
- Reproducibles 124

Conclusion 127

Index 128

INTRODUCTION

The Year That Inspired This Book

In the early days of September 2001, I set up a fourth-grade classroom at P.S. 89 in lower Manhattan. It was the most modern, the largest, and the brightest classroom I'd ever taught in, with views of the Hudson River and the Statue of Liberty. I had brand-new blackboards and whiteboards, plenty of storage, a fabulous library, an overhead projector, and air conditioning. I was expecting 24 children—a bigger class than I'd ever had while teaching in private school—and I had plenty of room for them.

Four days into the school year, on the morning of September 11, I was standing in the middle of the classroom waving a purple folder and asking children to come to the meeting area when the first of two planes hit the World Trade Center, three blocks downtown. Our ordinary, noisy morning turned nightmarishly tense and hushed as terrified, breathless parents began appearing at the doorway to pick up their children, unsure where to take them. Within an hour, the entire school community was evacuating the building and hurrying uptown along the Hudson River's bike path, in a sea of sirens and dazed office workers, as the North Tower collapsed behind us.

In the weeks that followed, P.S. 89 became a command center for search-and-rescue, then recovery, operations. Baskets of crayons and snap cubes were swept from classroom shelves and replaced with computer equipment, hard hats, and boxes of dust masks. Massive satellite maps of Ground Zero covered hallway murals and welcome signs. The lobby was covered in plastic sheeting and staffed by the National Guard. The playground was coated with dust.

My colleagues and I set up classrooms again—this time in very overcrowded quarters in another New York City public school. P.S. 3 accommodated us as generously as they could, but they didn't have much space to spare. My students and I shared a room with P.S. 89's other fourth-grade teacher, Margaret, and her class. We were more than 40 people in a room with almost no furniture, and we were lucky; there was another room holding close to 70 children.

Our city was in a state of perpetual anxiety and shock. Storefronts, lampposts, and newspaper boxes were covered with flyers bearing the faces of missing people. The roar of military aircraft became familiar. Almost without exception, our students and their families were unable to return to their homes and were instead camping out in hotels or the apartments of relatives or friends. No amount of preparedness or cheerfulness on the part of bewildered teachers could keep the chaos in the air from infiltrating the crowded classrooms. Those early days were almost unbearable.

As an experienced teacher, my ideas of how things *should* be short-circuited my imagination. Children should be at tables, not on the floor. They should be eating their lunches in a cafeteria, not on the rug. We should be able to pass out paper without stepping on people's fingers. This just wasn't school.

Margaret, a first-year teacher, got her bearings before I did. Her freshness as a teacher allowed her to address what was actually happening, instead of endlessly referencing what *should have* been happening. At her suggestion, we grouped the students into little families of four to six children, as if we were seating them at clusters of desks. Then we assigned members of the group tasks related to our basic needs as a class: distributing paper and supplies; collecting finished work and homework; cleaning up; sharing the group's ideas with the rest of the class.

We collected enough milk crates to create a supply cubby for each group. The crates allowed each group to access their notebooks, independent reading books, extra paper, pencils, and erasers quickly and easily, without creating traffic problems.

The level of tension in the room dropped precipitously after we introduced the groupings, jobs, and crates. As small as they were, these changes gave us a precious gift: a chance to feel productive—we could make a transition without lapsing into complete madness—and to begin to build community. School, as different as it still was from what we had all expected, became a source of what we all needed most: a little order in our lives.

A month later, we moved again, to a school with plenty of space and furniture to accommodate us, and a collection of donated supplies that had poured in from all over the country. We settled in there for the winter months. Finally, in late February, we returned to our classrooms at P.S. 89.

In the course of all the moving, I learned a lot about streamlining my work as a teacher. I learned how to stop generating so much paper clutter, to simplify my planning, to expect and accept changes in course, and to make everything portable. I also learned that the only indispensable part of a classroom is the spirit of the community that inhabits it.

When we returned to P.S. 89 in late winter of 2002, I brought my newly streamlined ways of working to our original classroom. In addition, whenever I felt overwhelmed, I asked myself questions like these:

- What is our central purpose in this lesson/activity/project?

- What do my students need most from this experience?

- How can I best balance the bottom line—my students' readiness for the next grade—with what I value most as a person?

Natalie Dean, an extraordinary teacher and close friend, suggested that other teachers might benefit from some of the concepts and systems I had developed during the course of this challenging year. Natalie's suggestion was the beginning of this book.

In the chapters that follow, you will find strategies for making teaching a more manageable, enjoyable, and satisfying job. All of the ideas in this book are intended to enhance the efficiency and productivity of your classroom so you can put your energy into the heart of your work.

I believe a collaborative spirit and shared sense of purpose is the bedrock of a successful classroom, and that creating a classroom that works well is a collective endeavor. Therefore, I've begun the book by offering strategies for creating a thriving classroom community.

In Chapter 2, you'll learn about an approach to time management and curriculum planning that allows you to balance your long-term goals with the day-to-day demands of your classroom. This portion of the book includes guiding principles, tools, and resources for ensuring that your planning is focused and realistic, and that you stay on top of those events—tests, curriculum culminations, parent conferences—that can make a mess of our careful planning.

Chapter 3 tackles the organizational challenges presented by our classrooms themselves. You'll have the opportunity to look at a variety of floor plans and read about other teachers' approaches to designing their rooms, and also to reflect on the impact of design choices on classroom life. With tools and ideas for clearing clutter, conserving materials, and involving your students in keeping the classroom in order, this chapter will guide you through the process of planning a room that will *stay* organized all year long.

In Chapter 4 you'll find a simple, sane system for managing all that paper your students produce (and ideas for reducing the amount they use in the first place). I also introduce strategies for keeping the kind of records that inform your teaching and make conferring and report-writing efficient. Finally, Chapter 4 offers guidelines for successful parent conferring.

As you read about ways to create community and manage time, space, and paper, you'll notice common themes. These principles are at the heart of *Your Best Year Yet!*

- Know yourself as a teacher, above and beyond what others expect of you. Be clear about what matters to you.

- Long-term priorities and immediate concerns need to be balanced and rebalanced—every day.

- Make room for change. Invite it. Welcome it.

- Begin cultivating student investment and involvement in classroom life on the first day of school, and continue to do so all year.

Ultimately, the goal of this book is to help you build the kind of classroom you will enjoy walking into each morning: one that is orderly and efficient and yet inspires, delights, and surprises you.

Look for this symbol throughout the book, indicating an opportunity for student participation in maintaining the classroom.

CHAPTER 1

The Foundation of a Classroom That Works:

Creating a Classroom Community in the Upper Grades

A teacher can't build an excellent classroom alone. Fortunately, teachers get to collaborate with children, the world's most energetic workforce. Since children gain invaluable experience by working with their teacher to build a classroom, and since they are deeply invested in the success of their efforts, it makes sense to engage them in this challenging, rewarding, year-long process.

Unlike kindergartners and first graders, who glow with first-day enthusiasm just about every morning of the year, upper-elementary students scrutinize the teacher and classroom environment thoroughly before deciding whether to put much energy into school life. They're tougher to engage, and they won't trust their teacher automatically.

What makes the difference for these eight- to eleven-year-olds? Simply put, their contributions need to matter: Their ideas need to be heard and discussed; their inventions need to be tested; their work needs to change the room; and their absence needs to have an impact on the community.

When upper-elementary children feel a sense of genuine responsibility—in addition to the confidence that they are appreciated as individuals and that their needs will be met—they become enthusiastic contributors to classroom life. Your students will be highly motivated to do their share if the classroom is truly a *community*, one that nurtures its members and is sustained by them.

Once a classroom community begins to evolve, it needs to be cultivated, nourished, and (inevitably) repaired. Students will need ongoing opportunities to learn *how* to be skilled contributors, supporters, collaborators, and negotiators. As teachers, we can provide these opportunities every day by modeling the behaviors we want to encourage in our students, and by demonstrating through our choices and actions that we recognize, trust, and expect the best from each one of the children we teach.

The Nuts and Bolts of Building Community

The recommendations that follow are all positive ways to promote a sense of belonging, pride, confidence, and agency in your students. Read on for guiding principles for creating community, and ideas for bringing the principles to life in your room.

✱ Let students speak for themselves.

Model good listening. Learn to provide strong leadership without overwhelming students with your own ideas and intentions.

> **EXAMPLES**
> - When a child is having difficulty presenting an idea, ask questions until he or she can clarify it independently, rather than correcting him or her or restating it yourself.
>
> - When children have conflicts with one another, view yourself as a mediator rather than a judge. Help children express their feelings and needs clearly and appropriately, and encourage them to speak directly to one another.

✱ Consider your students' healthy social and emotional development to be part of your responsibility as a teacher.

You are only *part* of the picture, of course, but if you have your students' respect, you can make a big difference in their lives.

> **EXAMPLES**
> - Help children understand the impact of their behavior on others. Instead of telling a student, "That's not nice," ask, "How do you think she feels when you talk to her like that?"
>
> - Offer a genuine apology when you've made a mistake: "I'm sorry, Robbie, you're right—you did turn in your homework on time. I should have checked the pile twice."
>
> - Let students know you notice—and care about—how they treat one another. Never ignore situations in which a child is being taunted, isolated, or bullied. If you're not sure how to address the situation, seek help from an experienced colleague, administrator, or school psychologist.

✱ Make everyone a star.

Notice what each of your students does well. Tell children precisely, and publicly, if appropriate, what it is that you notice. If you have students who struggle to find success, find opportunities in which you know they'll succeed.

> **EXAMPLE**
> During a week of writer's workshop, you might make a point of focusing on struggling students, those who don't consider themselves good writers. Find a bright spot in a child's work—for example, an unusual word choice, a surprising comparison, or an original story opener. After getting the student's permission, talk to the class: "I'm so sorry to interrupt your work, but I just have to share Sarah's beautiful description of her grandfather's voice. Sarah, would you like to read this yourself, or may I read it aloud?"

✱ Provide a variety of contexts for schoolwork.

Some people thrive in partnerships or small groups, some shine in large groups, and some do their best work alone. Consider all the possibilities for configuring the community during the course of each day so everyone gets a chance to succeed, and to stretch.

> **EXAMPLE**
> As you finalize your schedule for each school day, take a moment to ask yourself whether there are opportunities for a variety of working configurations. Make it a goal to offer a variety of experiences each day. (For ideas, see page 48, Balancing the Days.)

✱ Offer your students *real* responsibilities and opportunities for leadership.

Every child should participate in building and maintaining the classroom. Whether your students are responsible for watering the plants, distributing homework to classmates, or reporting on current events, make your expectations clear and provide opportunities for children to learn the skills they need to meet those expectations.

Beyond issuing reminders, don't do students' jobs for them unless health or safety is at stake. Rescuing students from their responsibilities undermines their learning and sends the message that they aren't competent. When necessary, adjust the nature of a leadership or helping task to suit the abilities of a child, to ensure that he or she can be successful.

> **EXAMPLES**
> - Teach students where things belong and how they're organized, and expect them to take care of the room as well as any plants and animals living there.
>
> - When a new student enters your class midyear, assign a new "buddy" every day for a week to ensure that he or she knows how the classroom works, has company for lunch and recess, and has numerous opportunities to become part of the social life of the classroom.

✱ Talk openly about differences, and model respectful language for doing so.

Demand and *model* inclusion and tolerance in your classroom.

It's a cliché because it's true: Children will mimic what you do, not what you say. Telling students to "be nice" may affect a momentary change in their behavior, but it will never affect their beliefs or challenge their assumptions. When students hear about your experiences, witness your generosity, and believe that your heart is open to all of them, they will be inspired and they will *grow*.

> **EXAMPLE**
>
> Eli arrives for school with his mom, who also has Eli's brother in tow. Eli's brother, Jake, has Down's syndrome. As Eli says goodbye to his family, I overhear another student, Rodger, make a quiet joke about Eli's brother. I pull Rodger aside, out of Eli's earshot, and speak to him, repeating his words precisely, and asking him to explain what he meant. "Rodger, I heard you call Eli's brother a 'retard.' Tell me about that word. What does it mean to you?"
>
> After listening to Rodger, I let him know that the language he used is derogatory and hurtful, and that it does not do a good job of describing Jake. "I know a lot about Jake," I tell Rodger, "because I've asked Eli. I know that he is five years old, that he goes to school and plays soccer, that he loves to draw, and that he was born with Down's syndrome. Down's syndrome changes the way people look and think and talk. I know some things about Down's syndrome because someone in my family has it, too. Are you curious about it? We can talk more about it if you like."
>
> Once I've offered Rodger this opportunity to express his curiosity or discomfort, I also create a firm boundary. "Now that you understand that the word you used is hurtful, I expect that you won't use it again—whether I'm listening or not. In this classroom, we treat one another with kindness. Do you have any questions for me, or is this settled?"

A Class Journal

Keeping a Class Journal, in which your students will take turns recording each week's most memorable events, is a great way to cultivate a sense of shared history. Provide some clear instructions and guidelines for writing in the journal (I glued the instructions shown at right onto the inside front cover), and give it to a new student each Monday so he or she can write about the week's events.

Each week's writer should read his or her entry aloud to the class once it's finished. It's also fun to include a photo of each week's author, perhaps accompanied by an artifact related to his or her entry. Make sure the journal is in school for at least one or two days each week, so students can enjoy remembering the year's events and accomplishments.

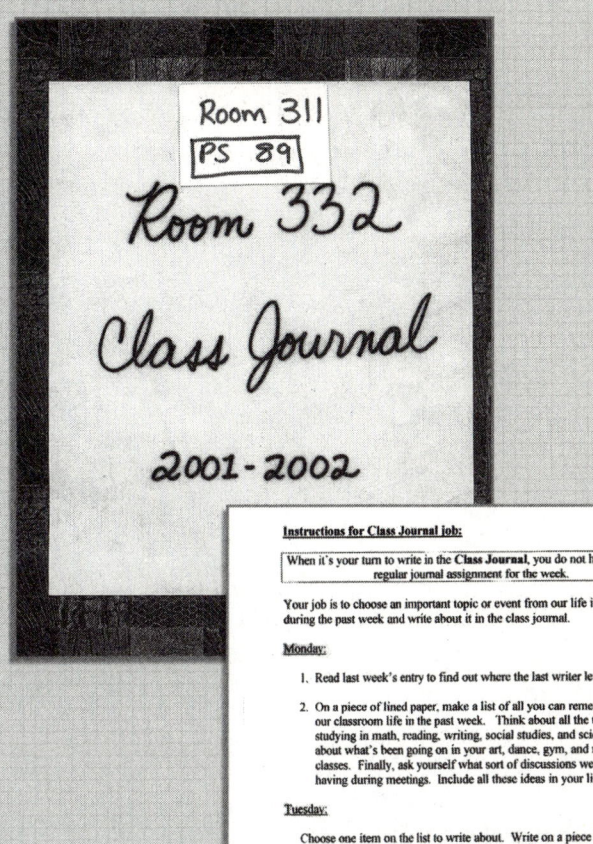

CHAPTER 1: The Foundation of a Classroom That Works

✱ Make sure children understand what's expected of them, and that they have the skills for accomplishing those tasks.

Never assume students have mastered a skill you haven't taught. Everything from how to argue respectfully to how to operate a three-ring binder may need to be explicitly taught.

> **EXAMPLE**
>
> Every Friday, you expect your students to clean out their desks. While some students may have had plenty of experience organizing their belongings, others may need both instruction and practice.
>
> Teach this and any other skill incrementally, breaking it down into steps. For instance:
>
> (1) Remove everything from your desk.
> (2) Throw away anything that is no longer useful.
> (3) Return anything you've borrowed from the classroom or from other students.
> (4) Put everything else back into your desk neatly.
>
> It can be very useful to list and illustrate these steps for your students—either on chart paper, as a poster for the whole class, or on regular-sized paper that can be stored in a "how-to" binder students can access anytime.

✱ Celebrate.

Find numerous opportunities during the year to enjoy what you and your students have accomplished together.

Teachers are often reminded that it's the *process*, not the *product*, that matters most. While there is plenty of truth in that idea, the prospect of an audience for their finished work (even if it's simply their fellow students) surely inspires students and allows them to enjoy hard-earned appreciation for their efforts.

> **EXAMPLES**
> - Design curriculum culminations that involve parents or the larger school community: museums of children's work, storytelling festivals, costumed re-creations of historical events, exhibits of science experiments, poetry readings, and publishing parties.
> - Make a point of inviting people into the room during ordinary days, too, to show them your students' work.

Although it certainly involves significant effort on your part, investing in your students' social and emotional health will enrich your school year in ways nothing else can. Moreover, this investment will make your job easier: Children who are supported and challenged appropriately will offer you their energy and cooperation in creating a classroom that works.

Recommended Literature on Children's Social and Emotional Growth

Interested in reading more about how to support your students socially and emotionally? Here are a few resources, which are well-researched and accessible to teachers:

- Cohen, J. (Ed.). (2001). *Caring classrooms/ intelligent schools: The social emotional education of young children.* New York: Teachers College Press.

- Ellison, L. (2001). *The personal intelligences: Promoting social and emotional learning.* Thousand Oaks, CA: Corwin Press.

- Elias, M. (Ed.) et al. (1997). *Promoting social and emotional learning: Guidelines for educators.* Alexandria, VA: Association for Supervision and Curriculum Development.

- Watson, L. E., Ecken, L., & Kohn, A. (2003). *Learning to trust: Transforming difficult elementary classrooms through developmental discipline.* Hoboken, NJ: Jossey-Bass.

Also see www.csee.net, the Web site of the Center for Social and Emotional Education, for information about projects and training institutes currently available to educators.

CHAPTER 2

Purposeful Planning & Tools for Managing Time

By 8:30 in the morning, teachers are already juggling more bits of information than some people manage in an entire work week. Plans for five or six separate lessons are occupying a significant amount of space in your brain. You've probably been thinking through those lessons and creating or gathering materials for them since at least yesterday. Meanwhile, as children (and perhaps their parents) enter your room, you're issuing reminders, offering encouragement, mediating conflicts, making mental notes to contact this parent or that tutor, figuring out whose homework or permission slip is missing, answering phone calls from the office, filling out the attendance form, and taking a poll to find out who's having school lunch or taking the bus home.

And while you do your best to keep track of it all, you are also striving to keep your manner pleasant and gentle, your language clear and appropriate, your eye on the clock, your ear out for trouble—and your room in decent order.

It's easy to see how ideas, projects, goals, and deadlines begin to slip through the cracks, or how curriculum night, parent conferences, or standardized tests can sneak up on you and throw you into a panic.

The Challenge for Teachers

Teachers tend to adapt to the demands of curriculum planning in one of two ways. Some teachers resign themselves to living a fairly chaotic existence. They tend to focus closely on one day at a time, a perspective that has some clear advantages. Students benefit from being able to work at a comfortable pace, and—at least initially—each question, problem, unit, or investigation gets thoughtful attention. On the other hand, when a deadline looms and time runs short, projects may remain unfinished, and some parts of the curriculum may get hurried or skipped, shortchanging students' long-term academic goals.

Other teachers concern themselves so much with the constraints of the schedule or the calendar that, while everything gets "done" on time, it becomes difficult for them to respond to—or even notice—their students' diverse needs. This method focuses on students' *hypothetical* progress towards curriculum goals, and does not take into account their *actual* progress.

Fitting your plans into a daily schedule can be surprisingly challenging. Planning well requires that teachers balance long-term goals, immediate priorities, and time constraints while remaining sensitive to the needs of learners.

> Friday, September 23
>
> 8:30 Good Morning Time
> 9:00 Meeting
> 9:10 Wood/A   Science/B
> 9:50 Snack with Tim
> 10:10 Gym
> 10:50 Writing
> 11:40 Story
> 12:00 Lunch with Tim
> 12:40 Math
> 1:25 Roof
> 2:05 Quiet Reading
>   Clean Up
>   Games
> 3:00 Dismissal

A System That Works

In this chapter, I describe an alternative solution to these very different—but equally unsatisfying—approaches to managing time. This system has three components: a Working Calendar, a Planbook, and Artifact Binders. In combination, these elements help you maintain your awareness of the big picture—your overarching goals for the year—without locking you into an unrealistically rigid march from one period, project, or unit to the next.

Used alone, any of these three provides an incomplete perspective for planning and tells only a patchy story of the year once it's over. Together, however, they keep the planning balanced and focused. At year's end, they provide an extremely rich resource for next year's planning.

The **Working Calendar** gives you a year-long perspective. It's designed to be flexible but spare; there isn't much room for detail. Instead, the Working Calendar provides you with the widest possible view of your year and curriculum goals. Using it to guide your weekly planning will help you remember your long-term goals and keep your priorities in order. (Pages 20–30 show you how to assemble and use this management time-saver. Reproducibles of the forms I use are included on pages 54–56 in this chapter.)

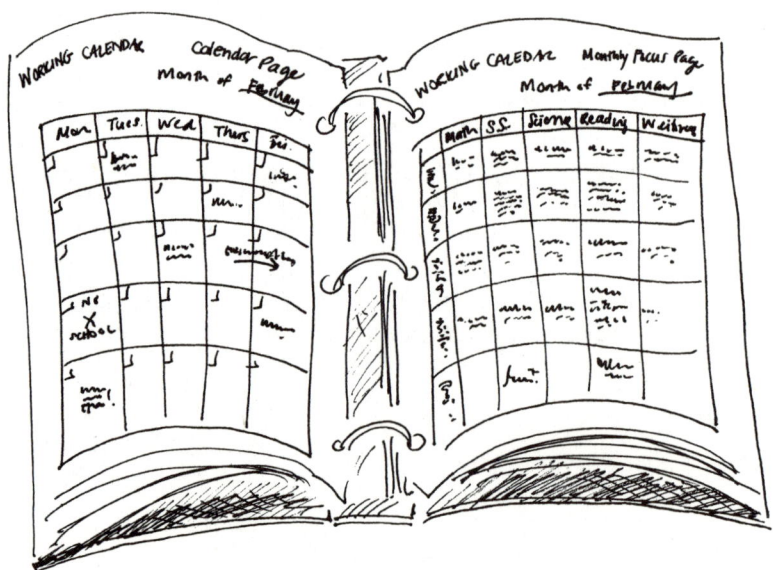

The time and care it takes to assemble a Working Calendar will pay off in increased efficiency throughout the year.

The **Planbook** is a place to schedule a day or a week at a time. A Planbook provides a necessary close-up view of life in your classroom on a daily basis, but it doesn't need to contain details of lessons or projects. This traditional teacher's tool is in fact for scheduling, not for detailed planning. (See pages 45–47 for fresh ways to use the Planbook as part of your planning system, including customizing your homemade or store-bought Planbook with additional forms and features designed to make your teaching life a little easier. Reproducibles of the forms I use are included on pages 57–61 in this chapter.)

Bring your enhanced Planbook home with you every day, and you'll always have access to the type of information—phone numbers for parents and tutors, lists of successful pairings or groupings of students— that makes your life easier.

Artifact Binders are like "museums" of your year. They are extensive records of the content, tools, and resources you use for each lesson, project, or activity. They may contain lesson plans, transparencies, samples of children's work, photographs of projects, lists of resources, bibliographies, and so on. The content of your Artifact Binders will evolve from year to year as your curriculum develops and changes. (See pages 49–51 for specific ideas to make artifact binders a useful planning tool.)

Artifact Binders couldn't be easier to maintain. A three-hole-punch and a five-minute commitment a day (at the most!) will provide you with a portable, current, easily accessed encyclopedia of your teaching year.

CHAPTER 2: Purposeful Planning & Tools for Managing Time 19

The Working Calendar, Backbone of Your Year-Long Plan

A Working Calendar is a durable, lightweight three-ring binder that contains your basic year-long goals for each curriculum area, as well as two forms for each month of the school year, the Calendar Page and the Monthly Focus Page.

The **Calendar Page** shows a full view of the month, and has room for basic schedule information, such as holidays, trips, or special events. It also includes very basic curriculum-planning information and reminders, such as "Begin Nonfiction Unit," "End Math Unit 1," or "Running Records, A–D".

WORKING CALENDAR — **Calendar Page**

MONTH OF ____October____

Monday	Tuesday	Wednesday	Thursday	Friday
	1 Reading: begin nonfiction unit	2 Curriculum Night	3	4
7 Start essays	8	9 Running Records, A–D	10	11
14	15	16 Running Records, E–P *Planning date for November	17	18 Ellis Island Trip
21	22	23 Running Records, R–Z	24	25 End Math Unit 1
28 Parent–Teacher Conferences in 2 Weeks	29	30 **Extra dance rehearsal Science: insulator experiments (final)	31 Halloween Dance Performance	

20   Your Best Year Yet!: A Guide to Purposeful Planning & Effective Classroom Organization

The **Monthly Focus Page** faces each Calendar Page. On this page, you'll detail your goals for the month (based on your yearly goals), and then list—very briefly—the kinds of projects, skills, tools, and strategies your students will need in order to meet those goals. There is also space on this form to note themes and connections among content areas—those that you plan to highlight and those that are discovered by your students as the year progresses.

The bottom part of this page is reserved for notes. These notes are intended to be very brief reflections on how your planning panned out. They will compose a realistic record of your progress in each curriculum area. This is necessary because what actually happens may be different from what you've planned—or because as you work your way through your plans, adjustments, improvements, or connections may occur to you. These notes, which can be very informal, are incredibly useful for refining next year's planning.

As you can see from the sample provided, writing space on this form is minimal for a reason: It's intended to keep you focused on your goals and prevent you from getting sidetracked by more incremental, day-to-day planning.

WORKING CALENDAR — Monthly Focus Page

MONTH OF __October__

	MATH	SOCIAL STUDIES	SCIENCE	READING	WRITING
GOALS	Packages and Groups unit, Investigations 1–3 (multiplication and division)	Build concept of "culture" Understand reasons for immigration; distinguish between immigrants and forced migrants (refugees, enslaved peoples)	Formulate questions; create hypotheses Collect, organize, and interpret data Explore concepts of "variable" and "control"	Develop nonfiction reading skills	Write persuasive essays
PROJECTS & ACTIVITIES	See book	1-year timeline: family rituals and celebrations Read oral histories and interview immigrants from our families Learn about slave trade via images/primary source material	Insulation experiments	Pose open-ended questions and figure out how to find answers Treasure hunts for information Research a topic using diverse sources: magazines, cookbooks, atlases, fiction	Use facts to support point of view; credit/cite sources Address opposing viewpoint Shape introductory and concluding paragraphs
STRATEGIES, SKILLS & TOOLS	See book	Interview skills: plan and ask questions, listen and follow up, take notes, turn interview content into narrative Draw inferences Gather data from primary source material	Work in small groups Create and interpret charts and graphs Use measuring tools	Differentiate between fact and opinions Use tables of contents and indexes to search for information Use children's search engine Skim, take notes, use graphic organizers	Engage the reader Use powerful verbs Back up opinions with facts and examples Use peer feedback Practice mechanics, editing skills
THEMES & CONNECTIONS				Find and use information. Use library resources to gather information	Facts vs. opinions
		Note-taking	Note-taking	Note-taking	
NOTES		More literature connections for slavery research?			Didn't seem ready for peer feedback— need more practice

CHAPTER 2: Purposeful Planning & Tools for Managing Time

Six Steps to Creating a Working Calendar

A Working Calendar provides you with the broadest possible view of the school year. Because maintaining this calendar involves referencing your long-term goals on a weekly basis, using it keeps your curriculum focused regardless of how many changes you make to your daily plans. In addition, the Working Calendar helps you stay aware of looming deadlines, anticipate important events, and pace yourself accordingly. A Working Calendar allows you to keep track of all curriculum areas in one place using a common, simple, and portable system. There are six basic steps to building a calendar, each one detailed below.

STEP 1 Gather materials.

To build a Working Calendar, you will need:

- a copy of the official school or district calendar, including all professional days, holidays, vacations, special events, and so on.

- dates for parent conferences, report cards, and standardized testing. Contact the main office of your school or district for any information you don't already have. (You may also find calendar information on the district's Web site.)

- a one-inch-thick three-ring binder.

- curriculum planning documents or teachers' guides to all published materials you will use. Separate them by curriculum area. (If two or more areas are truly integrated, there is no need to attempt to separate them.)

- one copy of the Calendar Page (page 54) for each month of the school year with the dates filled in. (Note: To save space, this calendar does NOT include weekends!)

- one copy of the Year-Long Goals form (page 55) for each area of the curriculum.

> **!** If you have a lot of flexibility in curriculum planning and scheduling, you may want to make two copies of your blank (dated) calendar. One of these calendars will serve as a rough draft. After you discover conflicts and make shifts or adjustments, you can make a cleaner version.

- one copy of the Monthly Focus Page form (page 56) for each month of the school year.
- a three-hole punch.

Optional materials:

- several boldly colored pencils or highlighters, each representing a different curriculum area
- a correction pen or brush-on correction fluid
- manila folders for organizing calendar materials
- dividers for the binder

STEP 2 Add basic calendar information.

Using a plain black pen, add all professional days, holidays, vacations, special events, and so on to your Working Calendar for the entire year. Mark holidays and vacations clearly by highlighting them or marking them with Xs. You should be able to tell at a glance how much teaching time you actually have for each month in your calendar.

Once you have marked in key events, go back and add early reminders to your calendar to give you lead time for these events. Consider adding more than one reminder for those dates that require special planning or preparation. My early-reminder list includes dates for parent conferences, report card deadlines, standardized testing dates, and all-school events that change the schedule or require extra preparation.

Put your completed Calendar Pages in a labeled folder and set them aside. You'll add more detail about curriculum in the steps that follow.

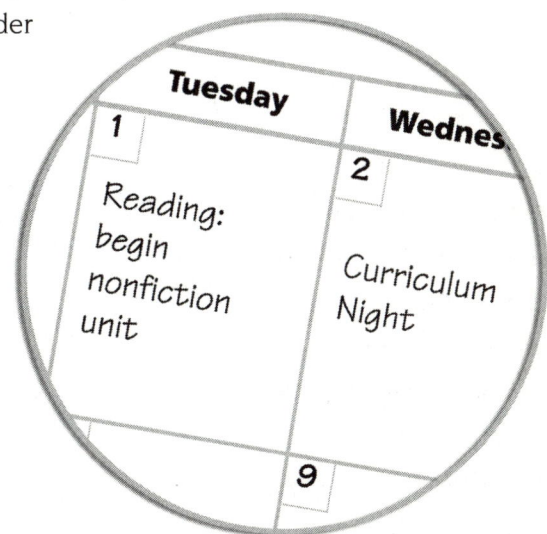

STEP 3 Determine year-long curriculum-area goals.

Depending on your particular teaching situation, you may have a set scope and sequence in every area of curriculum, or you may have plenty of flexibility in developing curriculum from year to year. Most likely, your teaching reality falls somewhere in between. Whatever the source of your curriculum, however, it's essential to be clear about your goals. The next phase of building your Working Calendar involves creating a **Year-Long Goals** form for each area of your curriculum. An example is provided on page 25.

Using the reproducible template on page 55, make a copy of the Year-Long Goals form for each curriculum area you'll cover and begin assessing your level of preparedness. Focusing on one curriculum area at a time, ask yourself:

- How well-planned is this area of curriculum?
- How flexible are unit dates and sequence?
- Are there any special events connected to this curriculum area that require extra time or preparation?

Address these questions in notes at the top of each form (hold off, for the time being, on the rest of the form). Here are some examples of how these notes might look for several different curriculum areas:

! **Since the Social Studies area is the most loosely defined and involves collaboration with other teachers, it's clear that developing this area of the curriculum is a major priority as I prepare to begin a new school year.**

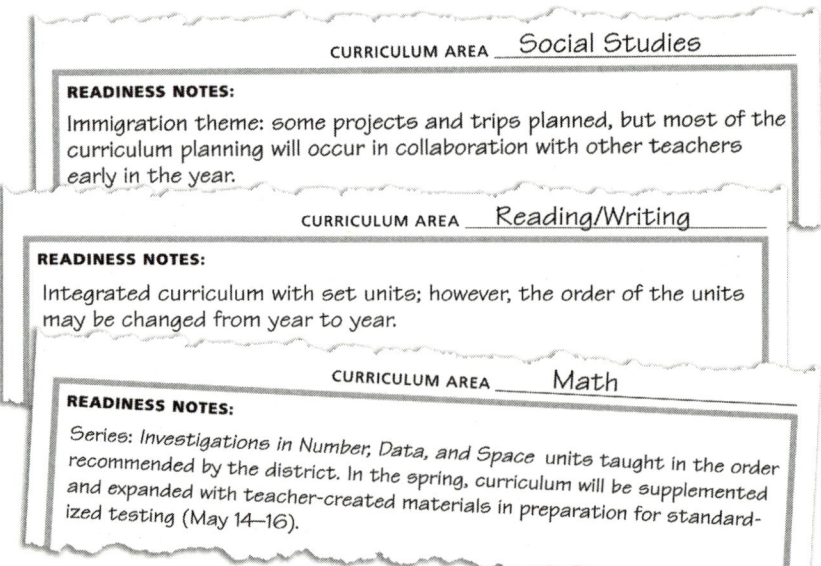

CURRICULUM AREA **Social Studies**
READINESS NOTES:
Immigration theme: some projects and trips planned, but most of the curriculum planning will occur in collaboration with other teachers early in the year.

CURRICULUM AREA **Reading/Writing**
READINESS NOTES:
Integrated curriculum with set units; however, the order of the units may be changed from year to year.

CURRICULUM AREA **Math**
READINESS NOTES:
Series: Investigations in Number, Data, and Space units taught in the order recommended by the district. In the spring, curriculum will be supplemented and expanded with teacher-created materials in preparation for standardized testing (May 14–16).

When your notes are complete, continue by filling out the remainder of each Year-Long Goals form. This form uses a simple approach to identifying goals. You are asked to identify what you want your students to:

- gain an understanding of (concepts, principles, connections).
- be able to do (skills, strategies, use of tools and resources).
- be ready for (curriculum culminations, deadlines, tests).

WORKING CALENDAR **Year-Long Goals**

CURRICULUM AREA: Social Studies

READINESS NOTES:

Immigration theme: some projects and trips planned, but most of the curriculum planning will occur in collaboration with other teachers early in the year.

Students will...

Gain an understanding of...	Be able to...	Be ready for...
concept of "culture"	locate countries on a world map	Ellis Island reenactment (April)
reasons for immigration	use maps, atlases, and globes	Immigration Celebration (June)
forced migration/slavery	distinguish between continents, countries, states and provinces, and cities and towns	
waves of immigration, 1600–2000		
diversity of immigrant experiences		
NYC's immigration history	find information in library, in books, on Internet	
development of immigrant communities	formulate questions to guide research	
US as a nation of immigrants	get factual information from literature	
family immigration history		
immigrants' contributions to American culture		

Complete the Year-Long Goals form first for those portions of the curriculum that are predetermined or well-established, since those can be completed quickly and set aside. In those areas in which you have more freedom and flexibility, the process may take a while; however, working through the form will support your planning process and save you time throughout the year. When you lose your way in weekly planning, you can always return to this form to refocus and remind yourself of your goals.

STEP 4 Sequence your goals.

Looking at your year-long goals for each curriculum area, decide which of your goals should be met early in the year, which of these can be addressed later, and which can be considered ongoing topics or investigations. Code your goals by writing E (early), L (later), and O (ongoing) beside each one, or by color-coding them with highlighters or colored pencils.

> **!** If any area of your curriculum is sequenced for you by a textbook or by administrative mandate, this part of the process is quick and easy. It will take longer if you are developing new curricula or sequencing curricula on your own. If you feel unsure about how best to sequence a more flexible portion of your curriculum, use the Curriculum-Building Resources on pages 31–44.

Students will...

Gain an understanding of...	Be able to...	Be ready for...
concept of "culture" E/O	locate countries on a world map E	Ellis Island reenactment (April)
reasons for immigration E	use maps, atlases, and globes E	Immigration Celebration (June)
forced migration/slavery E	distinguish between continents, countries, states and provinces, and cities and towns E	
waves of immigration, 1600–2000 O		
diversity of immigrant experiences O	find information in library, in books, on Internet O	
NYC's immigration history L	formulate questions to guide research O	
development of immigrant communities L	get factual information from literature O	
US as a nation of immigrants E		

E = Early   L = Later   O = Ongoing

STEP 5 Create monthly focus pages.

The first row of each Monthly Focus Page is reserved for Goals. Working with one curriculum area at a time, write the goals from your Year-Long Goals page in the appropriate Goals box on each Monthly Focus Page. Start with those goals you've marked with an **E** (early), and follow up with those labeled **O** (ongoing) and **L** (later). When you've worked your way through the whole school year, start over with the next curriculum area.

As you decide on goals for each month, examine the calendar carefully and make sure you're being realistic about the amount of time you're providing for each set of goals. Some months, for instance, have significantly less teaching time because of vacations or special events. Others may be dominated by test preparation or a special project, like a science fair.

Completing the Goals section of the Monthly Focus Pages is a huge step—they form a basic blueprint for a whole year's teaching and learning. Now lay each Monthly Focus Page beside the corresponding Calendar Page. Guided by your monthly goals, add basic curriculum dates to the Calendar Pages (for example, "Begin Biography Study" or "End Math Unit 4").

After reading this step, complete the next *one to two* months' focus pages in their entirety. Then add planning dates to your Working Calendar. For example, you might make the second Monday of each month your planning date for the following month.

Using Monthly Focus Pages

The Monthly Focus Pages ask you first to state your goals for each month, then explore them from several perspectives: Strategies, skills, and tools, projects and activities, and themes and connections. Here are some tips for addressing each area on the form.

! If you are planning an entire school year from the beginning, refer to The Natural Shape of a School Year (pages 37–41) to help you make decisions about timing your goals. Also, check out The Skills and Tools Approach to the Early Days and Weeks of the Year (pages 42–44).

STRATEGIES, SKILLS & TOOLS

Strategies, skills, and tools include what we actually do and use as we work to reach our goals. For instance, if we are writing persuasive essays, we may be using these strategies:

- engaging the reader with a compelling opening paragraph
- using powerful verbs to strengthen our sentences
- backing up our opinions with facts and examples
- making adjustments to our work in response to peer feedback

as well as these skills:

- beginning and ending paragraphs appropriately, and indenting properly
- using script handwriting, or typing on a computer
- citing our sources
- editing our own work

and these tools:

- a dictionary and thesaurus
- nonfiction books and Internet resources
- an editing checklist

PROJECTS & ACTIVITIES

When we choose projects and activities, we are addressing the question, "How will we meet our goals?" In what context will we learn new strategies, practice new skills, and use new tools?

Projects may range from the very short term (creating a graph that compares the heights of fourth graders to eighth graders, or reorganizing the classroom library on a Friday afternoon) to the long term (interviewing several family members and compiling an oral history, or planning, writing, revising, editing, publishing, and distributing a class magazine).

All projects and activities, regardless of scope, must be purposeful in order to be successful. They are not ends in themselves; they

---

! As you work on your Monthly Focus Pages, remember that your timing is very likely to shift as the year progresses. The framework you're creating now will help you stay focused and aware of your priorities. With the framework in place, you can afford to be flexible and spontaneous as you plan individual weeks and days.

Planning in too much detail too far ahead will result in one of two problems: Either your determination to stay on track will interfere with your ability to be flexible and responsive to your students, or you will find yourself spending too much time adapting or re-creating plans.

provide the *context* for gaining new tools, skills, and strategies and a means for reaching our goals. Have you ever seen a child work for hours on a magnificent piece of artwork, only to accidentally leave it in his or her cubby at the end of the day or tell you, "You can have it"? It's not that the final product doesn't matter; of course it does. But it was *the process of creating it*—making decisions, confronting obstacles, and practicing new skills—that helped the student grow.

THEMES & CONNECTIONS

In identifying themes, we are considering the concepts that unify our curriculum and the universal truths we touch through curriculum content, whatever it may be. The themes we find, or choose to cultivate, should address the developmental needs of our students and be visible in their everyday experience. Your curriculum content may contain many concepts related to conservation, innovation, or exploration, for example. You may decide to make this theme explicit, wait for your students to discover it, or use it to guide your choices or inspire your curriculum development.

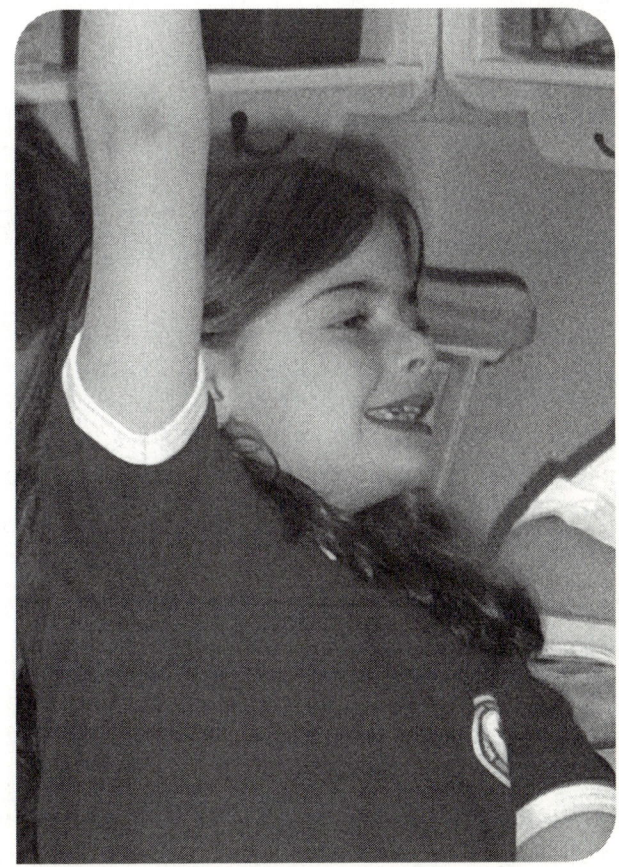

Connections are like sparks or synapses. They enliven curriculum and delight students, because they are proof that what is happening in school is relevant and true. It's a wonderful moment when, in the middle of a math discussion, a child makes a connection to a literary event or a concept explored in the social studies curriculum. These moments of connection allow students to build concepts from isolated bits of understanding. A student who makes such a discovery often feels empowered, as if he or she has unlocked one of the great mysteries of the adult world.

Making connections to concepts sparks student participation.

STEP 6 Assemble your working calendar.

When you've gathered and filled out the calendar and focus pages for your Working Calendar, you're ready to put together the binder. Three-hole-punch the Calendar Pages on the right side and the Monthly Focus Pages on the left side, so you can open your binder and look at each month from two perspectives.

Keep your Year-Long Goals forms in a separate section of the front or back of the binder, marked with a divider so they can be found quickly and easily.

Be Flexible, Yet Stay on Course

Now that you've created a month-by-month map of your year, you're ready to customize a Planbook and begin to schedule one or two weeks at a time. Remember that your monthly plans *are going to change*. Keep these two things in mind:

- Whenever you find that your monthly plan needs adjusting, return to your Year-Long Goals form. When you make changes, try to stay within the parameters of your original vision for the year.

- Resist the temptation to do very detailed weekly or daily planning too far in advance. Shifts in your schedule or your students' needs will, inevitably, make it necessary to rethink long-term plans.

! For ideas on planning assessment and integrating it into your Working Calendar, see Chapter 4.

Curriculum-Building Resources

If you have the opportunity to develop curriculum for your class or grade, you are in a position to provide your students with experiences truly tailored to their needs and interests. You also have a chance to think through curriculum content and learning processes in ways that will be invaluable to your professional development. As promising as this sounds, however, creating new curriculum can also feel daunting and overwhelming.

While a thorough discussion of curriculum development is beyond the scope of this book, the ideas that follow will help you set priorities, take advantage of available resources, and master the art of good curriculum timing. They will also help with the process of refining and improving upon your existing plans.

Guiding Questions provides the opportunity to identify resources and limitations, articulate your values, and develop a unified vision for your classroom.

Using Standards offers ideas for how to take advantage of established standards and use them imaginatively.

The Natural Shape of a School Year is a guide to predicting the rhythms of a school year, and making the most of each month—academically and within the social environment of your classroom.

The Skills and Tools Approach to the Early Days and Weeks of the Year provides strategies and activities to help you plan a high-energy, purposeful opening to the school year.

Guiding Questions

If you are a new teacher, working in a new school, or developing curriculum for a new grade level, try using the questions on these pages before you begin any curriculum-planning project. These guiding questions are intended to help you plan with an awareness of real-world limitations and constraints that can affect teaching style and curriculum content. In addition, the questions prompt you to locate the resources and support that already exist within your teaching community. Finally, they encourage you to articulate a unified vision of the school year based on your students' needs, your school's expectations, and your own values. Answering these questions probably won't take you more than 45 minutes or an hour at most, but doing so will save you time and hassle all year long.

* Do teachers at your grade level use any published materials—a math series, spelling series, or language arts series, for example? If so, can you supplement these materials? Will you receive any special training in using them? Can you re-sequence them for purposes of integration with other curriculum areas?

  _____
  _____
  _____
  _____

* In which areas of the curriculum will you have flexibility in scheduling, teaching methods, and/or content?

  _____
  _____
  _____
  _____

✱ Are you expected to show lesson plans to an administrator? How often? What form should they take?

___

✱ Are professional developers or other support staff available to help teachers plan and find resources?

___

✱ What opportunities exist for colleagues to plan and/or teach together?

___

✱ Does your school maintain a lending library of teachers' professional books?

___

RESOURCE PAGES

✻ In which curriculum areas do you feel most competent and confident as a teacher? Which ones make you nervous? Are there colleagues, specialists, or staff developers who may be able to mentor you in those areas?

_____

_____

_____

_____

✻ How familiar are you with children's literature for the age group you are teaching? Are experienced colleagues or the school librarian able to help you locate literature relevant to the academic or social goals of your curriculum?

_____

_____

_____

_____

> **!** One of my favorite sources of new children's literature is a newsletter published by the Flying Pig Bookstore in Vermont. The staff of this bookstore reviews children's literature with tremendous intelligence, sensitivity, and passion. Visit the store's Web site at www.flyingpigbooks.com, or contact them via e-mail at FlyingPig2@aol.com and ask to be added to their mailing list.

The following questions ask you to consider your priorities for the social and emotional life of the classroom. Yes, these goals are part of your curriculum! In fact, you will communicate your values and expectations for social development to your students through your actions, whether you've planned to "teach" them or not. Writing about your values will help you keep them in mind all year, and it will guide your decision-making in stressful times. When you write, make a list of values, beliefs, hopes, and goals rather than a list of rules.

* What are the central tasks for social development in children of your students' age?

  _____
  _____
  _____
  _____

* How do you want conflicts between students handled in your classroom?

  _____
  _____
  _____
  _____

* What are your expectations for your students' relationship with you? How do you want them to communicate with you? How do you want children to behave when they disagree with you about an idea or decision?

  _____
  _____
  _____
  _____
  _____

Using Standards

For new teachers especially, it's important to have access to a basic curriculum scope and sequence designed to address the most current thinking in education. High-quality standards provide invaluable guidance for teachers.

Standards are a very effective tool for focusing curriculum planning, managing time, and ensuring that assessment is thorough and fair. School and district standards generally take their cue from standards published by various national organizations such as the National Council of Teachers of Mathematics or the National Council of Teachers of English.

Depending on your level of expertise and autonomy, published standards can provide anything from a very literal, month-by-month guide to the school year to a rough curriculum map—indicating direction, suggesting sequence, and drawing your attention to landmarks that shouldn't be missed.

PLANBOOK — Using Standards to Assess Curriculum Plans

STANDARD — By the end of the school year, students are required to produce several types of writing:	How are the skills required to meet this standard addressed by the curriculum?	What project(s) will provide opportunities to produce the required artifact?	How will the standard be assessed?
Informational writing, such as a science or social studies report. This writing should include appropriate facts and details.	Mini-lessons during journalism unit in writing workshop will address the elements of good informational writing; weekly homework essays will provide practice with focused writing and mechanical elements such as paragraphing.	During journalism study, students will produce articles on a variety of issues relating to their school, community, and city.	Both student self-assessment and teacher's assessment will be included in writing portfolio with article. Both assessments will be based on a checklist of content, craft, and mechanical standards addressed during unit.
A response to literature, such as a book review. This writing should show an understanding of the book's story, setting, and characters.	Literature response journal will be used throughout the year; a portion of mini-lessons during reading workshop will focus on the elements of story.	Students will write two letters, fall and spring, recommending books to next year's fourth graders. Letters will refer thoughtfully to the book's story, setting, and characters.	Fall and spring letters will be examined together to compare their depth, thoroughness, and quality of writing. Both will be included in a writing portfolio.
A story, fictional or autobiographical. This writing should establish interesting characters and situations, and should include details and descriptions.	Reading and writing workshops will both need to address character development and relationships, conflict, artful description, use of dialogue, and other elements of fiction craft.	During immigration study, students will write a piece of historical fiction based on the lives of a family living in a Lower East Side tenement at the turn of the century.	Together, teacher and students need to develop specific criteria for assessing the stories and deciding when they're finished.

When used imaginatively, standards can be liberating to teachers. Our shared goal is to remain spontaneous and flexible in our teaching while staying committed to thoughtfully chosen goals. Let the standards articulate the goals and suggest the pace. Your students' energy will fuel your progress, and you can use all the resources at your disposal to navigate your own path.

For example, in the standards planning chart shown here, I've listed several standards for writing achievement in the left column. I've used three questions (at the tops of the other columns) to determine whether the standards can be met with existing plans and to identify holes or missing pieces. You'll find a reproducible template of this form on page 57.

The Natural Shape of a School Year

A traditional September-to-June school year has a natural shape. Each part of the year has its own assets and challenges. Taking this shape into account can make your planning far more effective, and can help you anticipate and avoid certain pitfalls of classroom teaching. On the following pages you'll find a grid listing these challenges and assets as well as strategies for savvy planning.

AUGUST, SEPTEMBER & OCTOBER

School begins with a burst of energy—for better or for worse—and then settles into a routine. Children are highly motivated and proud of their new grade level, but still identify more with the previous year than the current one.

ASSETS
- The classroom is full of fresh energy and a sense of potential.
- Children feel pride in their new grade level and are interested in pleasing the teacher.

CHALLENGES
- A classroom community is not yet formed.
- Students have limited skills and language for the academic tasks ahead.
- Old social baggage can intrude on a new year.
- Children are curious about limits and boundaries, and will test them.

STRATEGIES & IDEAS
- Use noncompetitive community-building activities to help establish a group identity.
- Include children in the design of the room; assign community jobs; make your values and expectations for the community clear.
- Introduce and practice skills, tools, and vocabulary that will support your students' learning throughout the year.

RESOURCE PAGES

NOVEMBER

Before too long, the social landscape of the previous year begins to dissolve, and a new one forms. With older elementary students, this process can be painful, and it may impact the learning environment significantly, requiring the supportive intervention of the teacher.

ASSETS
- Children are comfortable in their classroom environment.
- Students remain concerned about your opinion of them. They know they still have time to make a good impression on you.

CHALLENGES
- The upbeat, energetic quality of the first couple of months begins to fade.
- Cold or inclement weather can keep children indoors.

STRATEGIES & IDEAS
- Be involved in your students' social lives. Make it clear that you are concerned about the social environment of the classroom, and help make sure that every child is emotionally and physically safe.
- Provide opportunities for every child to shine. Make positive teacher attention public and negative attention (i.e., discipline) private.
- Help children understand that the quality of their classroom life is, in large part, up to them. Give them real responsibilities.
- Be sure you have a good backup plan in case recess is cancelled. Find engaging indoor activities that you can live with all year.

DECEMBER

As the holidays approach, excitement and tension in the air infiltrate the classroom. This energy can be put to good use—or it can interfere tremendously with progress.

ASSETS
- Students are immersed in projects in every curriculum area. They have new skills and abilities and are eager to demonstrate them to the larger school community, parents, etc.

CHALLENGES
- Children are energetic, but often anxious and unfocused.

STRATEGIES & IDEAS

- Acknowledge that although holidays can be wonderful, they can be stressful, too. Tell stories about your own family's holidays. Find sophisticated picture books that capture both the joy and complexity of the season—for instance, those that deal with issues of celebrating separately with divorced parents, or having a houseful of guests.

- Plan to finish several projects—publish student books and have a publishing party; finish a read-aloud; graph the results of an experiment and put them on display—before the winter vacation. When children return after the holidays, they'll enjoy both the sense of accomplishment and the fresh start.

JANUARY

The arrival of the new year usually brings a burst of new energy. Teachers and students are refreshed by vacation and relieved to return to the structure of school life.

ASSETS

- Students' skills are solidifying. They should now have a sense of community and shared history. Routines are established, but may need to be reviewed.

CHALLENGES

- All those projects completed in December mean that new momentum must be created for the spring semester.

- Cold weather can continue to keep children indoors.

- Children may be stuck in social "roles": the clown, the "bad" kid, the high-achiever.

STRATEGIES & IDEAS

- Keep up the pace of the curriculum.

- "Promote" children to new levels of responsibility. Give them more decision-making power where appropriate.

- Emphasize that everyone is making a fresh start. Don't carry grudges; give everyone some room to reinvent him- or herself.

FEBRUARY & MARCH

In both temperate and cold climates, a trying period begins. Children may spend a lot of time indoors and can become impatient with one another and their teacher.

ASSETS
- Students have many accomplishments behind them, and are beginning to watch older children carefully and wonder a little about "next year."

CHALLENGES
- The school year may have a "stale" feel.

STRATEGIES & IDEAS
- Help students take stock of all they've accomplished and then set goals for themselves for the rest of the semester.
- Be open, within reasonable limits, about your own personal goals.
- Surprise your students with occasional breaks in routine, like a homework-free night or a Friday afternoon movie.

APRIL & MAY

The arrival of spring vanquishes winter doldrums almost instantaneously. Even in warm climates, a school community is revitalized by the moment the end of the school year comes into view. It's not just the rush to get to the end that cheers us up; it's also the opportunity to take stock of all we've accomplished. And there's so much more to do!

ASSETS
- Summer's approach inspires and invigorates students. They are often cheerful about hard work, because the end is in sight.

CHALLENGES
- The curriculum can be very overwhelming and "packed" at this time of year. The days begin to fly by, and it often seems that too much is happening at once. Everything feels unfinished.

STRATEGIES & IDEAS
- Use the days before holidays and vacations to begin to finish projects or culminate pieces of the curriculum.
- Stay focused. Keep children aware of their personal goals and their progress toward them.
- Begin discussing what's in store next year for students. Be enthusiastic about students' accomplishments and serious about how much more work still needs to be done.
- Make room for projects and explorations initiated by your students.

MAY/JUNE

During the last month of school, classrooms tend to be bursting with the energy of the approaching summer—and with finished projects, special events, and curriculum culminations. The room feels a little looser; both students and teachers feel more relaxed and spontaneous. It's time to celebrate what you've finished together.

ASSETS
- The end of the year brings many opportunities for reflection.

CHALLENGES
- Children begin to experience anxiety about the end of the school year, and the changes and separations it will bring. They also worry about whether they'll be ready for next year.

STRATEGIES & IDEAS
- Provide opportunities for students to meet and interview next year's teachers and their current students. Be sure to prepare students carefully by engaging them in a class discussion beforehand, and allowing them to write down their questions about the following year so they won't forget them.

- Help students finish what remains unfinished. Even when students have lost interest in a project, finishing it can still make them feel proud.

- Invite parents, administrators, and other classes to view your students' finished work. Instead of simply sending work home, schedule an event—a publishing party, a portfolio party—to create some ceremony around it.

- Create a classroom graduation ceremony if children in your grade don't graduate formally. Make it relaxed, joyous, and inclusive. Acknowledge the year-long contributions and growth of every single student in terms that matter to each of them.

The Skills and Tools Approach to the Early Days and Weeks of the Year

The first day of school scares teachers just as much as it scares students. Students lie awake at night in the days and weeks before school starts, wondering, "Will I have any friends? Will I be able to do the work? Will my teacher like me?" Teachers lie awake, too, wrestling alternately with opposing worries: "How will I fill the time?" or "How will I get it all done?"

In my first few years as a teacher, it was the former question that worried me more. I was frightened of not having enough to do, of children finishing assignments too quickly and waiting for more. As the years went on and I developed a better sense of all that needed to happen in the course of a year, I was overwhelmed by the latter question.

I finally developed an approach to the first days and weeks of school that addressed both concerns. Using a very broad view of each curriculum area, I try to identify the underlying skills, strategies, tools, and vocabulary my students will need throughout the year, and to teach them during the early weeks of school. Even if I have only a basic idea of a part of the curriculum—for instance, I know we'll study the Inuit people in social studies, but I am unsure of the projects we'll do—I can think about skills used in any social studies curriculum: geography and mapping skills; research skills; museum skills; or concepts of culture or archaeology appropriate to the grade level.

I might also choose to introduce tools we'll use throughout the year: writer's notebooks, editing checklists, math manipulatives, thermometers and other measuring tools used for scientific investigations, etc. Students should learn these skills, strategies, tools, and vocabulary in the context of engaging, challenging projects. Examples and sample activities for the skills and tools approach will follow.

With a skills and tools approach, we begin the school year with lots on the agenda. From the first days, school feels substantive and purposeful to my students and to me. In addition, by practicing vital skills early on, we save time all year long.

> **!** Don't take the time now to create a *schedule* for the first days and weeks of school. Instead, create a *list of activities*. Wait to finish your long-term planning first, because it may inspire you to make changes. Creating a list of activities will reassure you that you've got plenty to do, and that it will be meaty and well thought-out. Remember—it's easy to manage time when you have a sense of purpose. It's harder to start with time to fill, and search madly for a way to use it!

Ideas and Examples for a Skills and Tools Approach

SOCIAL STUDIES

In social studies, students may need practice using maps, globes, and atlases for a variety of purposes throughout the year. They will very likely need to use research tools such as the school library catalog and the Internet with efficiency. If they haven't had much experience with reading for information or using the table of contents or index of books, they should acquire those skills, too. When these skills are introduced, new vocabulary will naturally accompany them.

Suggested social studies activities:

- Mini-lessons on the use of maps, globes, and atlases, and on how to search for information using those tools.

- "Bird's-eye view" drawings of classroom objects or the classroom itself to reinforce understanding of a mapmaker's perspective.

- Lessons on the uses of indexes, tables of contents, library catalogs, CD-ROMs, or the Internet can be followed by scavenger hunts for books or pieces of information using those tools.

- Designate a bulletin board for curriculum-related vocabulary, and ask students to be on the lookout for new or hard-to-spell words related to their studies. Make students responsible for neatly copying the words they find onto index cards and adding them to the board, and also for consulting the display for correct spellings as they write.

A student learns to use a globe in the first weeks of school.

WRITING

Depending upon your approach to writing, students may need introductions to or practice with writer's notebooks, essay-writing skills, editing checklists, dictionary use, peer-conferring skills, word-processing skills, and so on.

Suggested writing activities:

- If you are using writer's notebooks, "tour" your students through your own notebook. If you are enthusiastic and serious about your own writing, your students will feel excited and privileged to view your work. They will also want their own notebooks.

- Use whole-class activities to teach students basic editing techniques and symbols. An overhead projector and a set of colored dry-erase markers work well for this purpose. Students love to find mistakes.

- If your students are expected to learn certain structured forms of writing—essays, formal letters, etc.—introduce and practice these skills early. Take the time to break down the structure into steps, and practice each step.

ORGANIZING TIME AND MATERIALS

Teaching some basic organizational skills to your students will do wonders for their confidence in approaching new challenges. Get students into the habit of articulating their plans for a project before beginning to work on it, and offer strategies for managing time and paper.

Suggested activities for teaching organizational skills and strategies:

- Articulate and model an organized approach to a math problem that requires several steps. Show students how you keep track of your work. Establish the expectation that students plan before they search for an answer.

- Ask students to share strategies with one another. For instance, ask students: "How can you be sure all your homework is finished before you stop working for the day? When you're researching an idea using several sources, how can you organize the information you find?"

These ideas, and those that your own curriculum plans inspire, will provide you with a beginning collection of year-opening lessons. Consider keeping your plans for the first weeks of the year in a separate Artifact Binder (see pages 49–51 for more about Artifact Binders), and add to the binder throughout the year as new ideas occur to you.

Customizing a Planbook: Your Weekly Schedule

While the Working Calendar provides you with an awareness of long-term goals, your Planbook balances that perspective with the nitty-gritty of finite work periods, special classes, and recess breaks. The Working Calendar is for planning; the Planbook is for scheduling.

Recognizing the difference between planning and scheduling is key to staying both focused and flexible throughout the school year. Planning means establishing goals for your teaching and then deciding exactly how you'll lead your students toward those goals. Scheduling is a matter of fitting your plans into the time you have. If you try to schedule before you plan, you will lose sight of your long-term goals. If you plan but don't schedule thoughtfully, you may discover that your plans aren't realistic.

To avoid either of these pitfalls, you will literally put your Working Calendar and Planbook side by side as you make curriculum choices week by week.

Teachers' planbooks are easy to find in school and office supply stores or in educators' catalogs. However, I usually make my own, using a one-inch-thick binder and a very simple weekly form (provided as a reproducible on page 58). I also add some features and resources to my Planbook so I have frequently used materials at my fingertips. Should you choose to create your own or supplement your current planbook, you'll find the reproducible forms you need in this chapter.

In addition to the basic weekly planning form, your Planbook might include the following resources:

- a list of students, including their full names, birth dates, and parents'/guardians' names and phone numbers (page 59)

- a list of students who receive additional support (resource room, speech therapy, private tutoring, etc.), and contact information for support providers (page 60)

- lists of pairings or groupings used for specific projects, along with notes indicating which ones were successful and which ones weren't (page 61)

- adhesive library pockets for sticky notes, which are handy for jotting down scheduling ideas and reminders for an upcoming week

Long-Term Goals in Real Time: Using the Working Calendar and Planbook Together

When used together, the Working Calendar and Planbook balance the long-term goals you established at the beginning of the year with your ever-shifting week-to-week priorities.

Each month's Calendar Page serves to remind you of looming deadlines, new projects, and special events that affect your schedule. The accompanying Monthly Focus Page keeps you aware of your goals and specific ideas for reaching them. But a closer, day-to-day view is essential—and that's where the Planbook comes in.

For example, my October Calendar Page, shown below, has provided a reminder that a special event (a dance performance followed by a party) will take up some class time during the final week of the month. As I work around the scheduling constraints to create a plan for the week, the goals on the Monthly Focus Page help me set priorities.

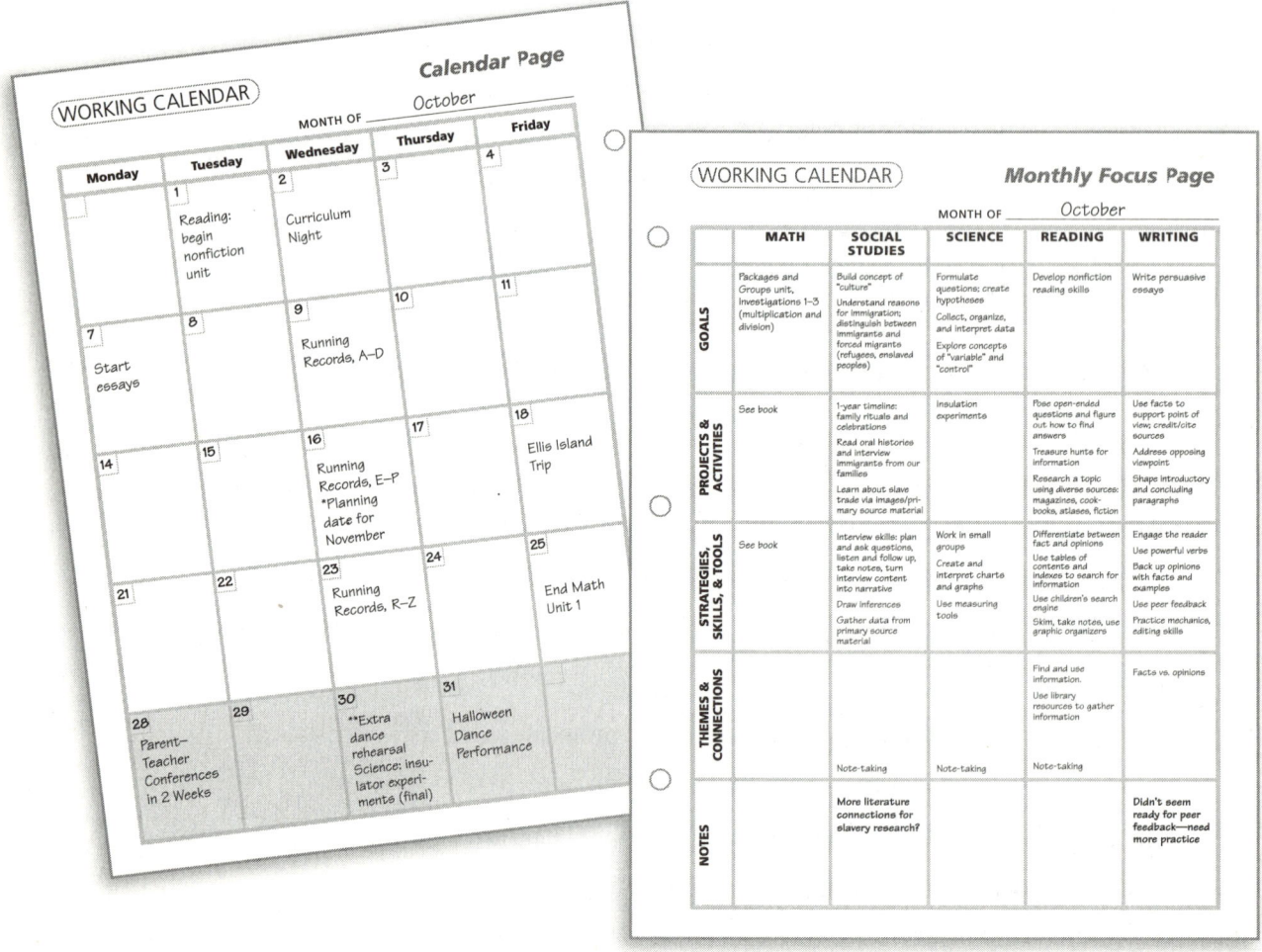

A Strategy for Planning the Week

Instead of scheduling one day at a time, schedule one curriculum area at a time, keeping your long- and short-term goals in mind. Try to be strategic about timing as well.

In the example, I take advantage of Monday morning, a high-energy, high-focus time in my room, to introduce a new math unit, and I give it a double period. Two other projects will require extended blocks of time this week: finishing our social studies time lines and building and testing the insulators we designed last week. I schedule each of these projects next to make sure they have adequate time.

I use the remaining time in the schedule for lessons, activities, and projects that require less time and/or do not have looming deadlines. I'm also keeping my eye on creating balance in the schedule (see page 48 for tips on balancing your schedule). Even though we usually do the read-aloud at the very end of each day, I'm adding two extra sessions—after gym on Monday and after the dance rehearsal on Wednesday—because I know that it's calming and focusing for my class after they've been very active. I know that the work that follows will be higher quality if I provide this transition.

PLANBOOK   **Week of** October 28–November 1

	Monday	Tuesday	Wednesday	Thursday	Friday
8:40	Math (begin unit 2)	Math	Library	Math	Math
9:20		Social Studies (time line)	Writing Workshop	Social Studies (time line)	Woodworking
10:00	Reading Workshop		Worktime	Writing Workshop	Writing Workshop
10:40	Science (building insulators)	Writing Workshop	Final Insulator Experiment		Read-Aloud
11:20		Read-Aloud		Art	Worktime
12:00	LUNCH	LUNCH	LUNCH	LUNCH	LUNCH
12:40	Gym	Reading Workshop	Dance Rehearsal	Dance Performance	Social Studies
1:20	Read-Aloud / Worktime	Community Service Projects	Read-Aloud		Lab Reports
2:00		Dance	Data + Conclusions for Insulator Experiments	Poetry	Independent Reading

CHAPTER 2: Purposeful Planning & Tools for Managing Time

Balancing the Days

After you fit all your plans for the week into the time you have, take a second look at each day. Give yourself and your students the best chance of having a satisfying, productive week by ensuring that your days are balanced. Ask yourself:

- Does the day include opportunities for students to work as a whole group, in small groups or partnerships, and individually?

- How will the demands of this day feel to your fastest, most efficient workers? How about your slower workers or struggling students?

- Is the day broken up by special classes or events? If it is, can you extend activities or projects into longer blocks, to eliminate transitions?

- Are there enough transitions (involving physical movement) in this day to keep it feeling varied and lively? Are there too many transitions, making the day feel choppy and rushed?

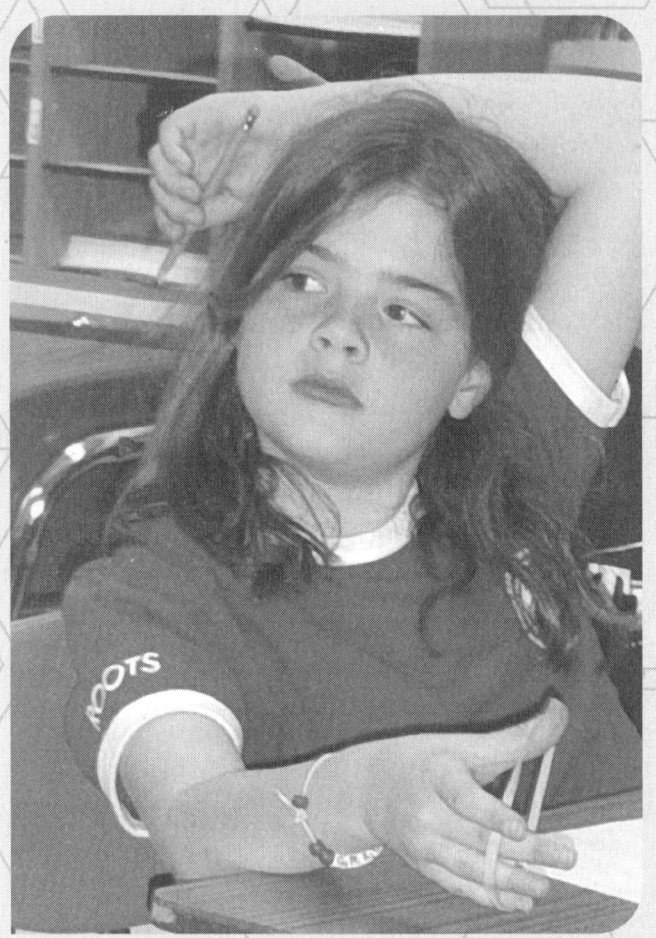

Know when students are ready for a break or a change of pace

Make changes to your schedule in order to create balance, if you have the freedom to do so. When you are not able to make such changes, your awareness of scheduling imbalances is still useful. Humor, patience, and understanding can go a long way toward helping students manage the anxiety created by numerous transitions or the frustration brought on by too much uninterrupted sitting.

As the school year progresses, look for patterns in your days, noting what works for your class. For instance, what sorts of activities seem to work best in the morning? Which ones work right after lunch? At the end of the day? Whenever possible, use these insights to inform your scheduling.

The Artifact Binder: A Place for Records and Resources

The Working Calendar describes the basic structure of the year: your goals, how you plan to reach them, and how your plans change as the school year progresses. It remains fairly portable because of what it does not contain: your detailed lesson plans, class-work and homework pages, samples of children's work, and teaching materials.

Those latter materials occupy Artifact Binders. Artifact Binders are *detailed records* of what happens each day of the school year. A separate three-inch-thick binder for each curriculum area evolves in tandem with the Working Calendar. Materials are kept in chronological order. If you think it will help you locate and file materials more easily, you can add dividers to the binder to mark months or semesters.

Artifact Binders should contain formal or informal lesson plans or teaching notes, copies of worksheets, teaching materials, overheads, homework, copies of important readings or resources, as well as samples of student work. You might include photos, sketches, and other teaching materials relevant to a lesson, placing them in a 9- by 12-inch envelope you've three-hole-punched. These materials are filed daily, dated, and kept in chronological order. In addition, when you file new materials or use old ones, write notes to remind yourself about what worked and what didn't ("This needed more time," or "Resources were harder to find than we thought. Visit the library first to make sure there are enough choices.").

The Artifact Binders quickly become heavy and full. Remember, they live in the classroom and don't need to be carted around.

! **For a full list of materials you might include in your Artifact Binder, see page 50.**

Artifact Binder contents might include:

- informal lesson plans.

- notes about success of mini-lessons and workshops as well as ideas for improvement (written on sticky notes and attached to the plans).

- teacher-created samples, worksheets, and homework.

- transparencies.

- examples of student work.

- chart-paper pages containing lists, sketches, graphs, etc. created by the class (folded and stored in large envelopes that have been three-hole-punched).*

- letters to parents explaining unit content and offering tips for helping with homework.

- reminders about where to find additional materials, such as those that are stored in a communal place or have been loaned to another teacher.

- photos of student work.

- photos of animals, landscapes, buildings, etc., relevant to the curriculum.

- explanatory labels from displays of student work.*

- poetry, excerpts of books, and samples of student writing that are useful year after year.

- planning documents, relevant phone numbers, notes, maps, and student materials related to class trips (stored in large envelopes labeled with the name of the trip).

*Remember to store only those items that are likely to be useful again.

> **!** **Consider keeping a separate Artifact Binder to record and store artifacts from the first days and weeks of school. For more on preparing for this important time, see The Skills and Tools Approach to the Early Days and Weeks of the Year, pages 42–44.**

Keeping Artifact Binders Current

An Artifact Binder is both a planning tool and a record-keeping system. Its contents will change throughout the year as you add or eliminate resources or change the order of units, projects, or activities. At the end of the year, it is a record of exactly what you did with your students—nothing more, nothing less.

As you begin a familiar unit, work your way through last year's plans, notes, and materials, adding to them or reshuffling them to reflect *the most current version* of your curriculum. If you find a better approach to a particular goal, you can toss the old one (or file it in a folder marked, for example, "Unused from Social Studies binder, 2003–2004"). If you don't touch it again in another year, it should definitely go into the recycling bucket.

Binders are preferable to filing cabinets or file boxes because they keep information visible and accessible, and because they make it easy to keep materials in chronological order. In the course of a hectic school day, it's very easy to toss things into file drawers or shove a file back in the wrong place, creating a mess you'll eventually need to address. It's also easy to forget what's in your filing cabinet; when you use a binder, you flip through old work all the time.

A good Artifact Binder collection can bring order to chaos.

Summary

Artful planning takes practice. When timing doesn't work out as you'd expect, use your Working Calendar and Planbook to make thoughtful decisions about how to proceed. First, record your thoughts about your original plan in the Notes section of a Monthly Focus Page—at the very least, you can save yourself some frustration next year.

Then return to your Year-Long Goals forms. Remind yourself of how the current project fits into the context of the whole year, and decide how best to reconfigure your plans.

Adjustments to consider include:

- **Changing the original time frame:** How vital is this project to your students' experience this year? Will extending or accelerating the time frame help keep you aligned with your original goals for the whole year?

- **Borrowing and bartering:** Does it make sense to make some exchanges in your long-term planning? Can you borrow time from a future project, or make a trade?

- **Rethinking the schedule:** If you are falling behind, look at your Planbook. Are you using low-productivity time for a project that requires a great deal of focus and energy? (See A Strategy for Planning the Week, page 47.)

- **Changing your expectations for the outcome:** What are your main priorities for this project? Rethink your planning according to what is most important in the process of completing the project, rather than focusing on finishing it.

One adjustment I would not recommend is lowering your standards in order to get something "done." Neither you nor your students will reap any benefit from this choice, because it compromises the integrity of the work. Imagine that an artist has set out to paint a landscape while the sun shines. She makes many sketches, experiments with color, and roughly sketches her plan on the canvas before beginning to paint. As the sun begins to set, she realizes she is far from finished. She has several choices: She can leave the work unfinished; she can stop working and return to the work at a later time; or she can hurriedly paint over her sketches just to finish up. By finishing in a hurry, she makes the most important part of her work—that which was done with patience and care—invisible.

Recommended Resources

Grant Wiggins and Jay McTighe have created a model for curriculum development they describe as "backward design," because it begins with the *understandings* that teachers want students to gain from a study. To read more about this powerful approach, check out these resources:

- **Wiggins, G. & McTighe, J. (2005). *Understanding by design*. Alexandria, VA: Association for Supervision and Curriculum Development.**

- **Understanding by Design Exchange**
  www.ubdexchange.org

To learn about national standards and access additional resources for teachers, investigate these sites:

- **National Council of Teachers of Mathematics**
  http://standards.nctm.org

- **The National Council of Teachers of English**
  www.ncte.org

- **National Council for the Social Studies**
  www.socialstudies.org

- **National Science Teachers Association**
  www.nsta.org

WORKING CALENDAR

Calendar Page

MONTH OF _____

Monday	Tuesday	Wednesday	Thursday	Friday

WORKING CALENDAR

Year-Long Goals

CURRICULUM AREA _____

READINESS NOTES:

Students will...

Gain an understanding of...	Be able to...	Be ready for...

WORKING CALENDAR

Monthly Focus Page

MONTH OF _____

	MATH	SOCIAL STUDIES	SCIENCE	READING	WRITING
GOALS					
PROJECTS & ACTIVITIES					
STRATEGIES, SKILLS & TOOLS					
THEMES & CONNECTIONS					
NOTES					

Using Standards to Assess Curriculum Plans

STANDARD	How are the skills required to meet this standard addressed by the curriculum?	What project(s) will provide opportunities to produce the required artifact?	How will the standard be assessed?

PLANBOOK

Week of _____

	Monday	Tuesday	Wednesday	Thursday	Friday

Student Information

STUDENT	BIRTH DATE	PARENTS/GUARDIANS	CONTACT INFORMATION

Students Receiving Supplemental Support

Student	Support Received/Contact	Support Received/Contact	Support Received/Contact	Notes

 *Groupings*

PROJECT: _____

GROUPINGS	NOTES

CHAPTER 3

Designing a Classroom That Will Stay Organized

This symbol indicates a specific strategy for involving your students in creating and maintaining the classroom.

Learning is messy. Organizing a classroom is not about making things tidy; it's a matter of creating systems that function smoothly and facilitate both teaching and learning. The pursuit of perfect order can undermine teaching and learning just as easily as can chronic disorder. In a well-organized classroom, both teacher and students understand the "mechanics" of their days—routines, expectations, responsibilities, decision-making processes—and do their share. A classroom is well organized if is both functional and pleasant to inhabit day after day.

This chapter will guide you through the process of setting up a classroom that will serve you and your students well all year. Look for the open-hand symbol shown here to find strategies that involve your students in creating and maintaining the classroom. Sharing responsibility with your students not only makes your job easier, it is also extremely beneficial to your students. (For more on why this is, refer to Chapter 1, The Foundation of a Classroom That Works.)

When you create your classroom, work from big to small. If you work through this chapter in the order it's presented, you will begin by making decisions about the arrangement of furniture in your room, then follow by organizing classroom materials. This may sound obvious—you can't put your markers on a shelf that's not there—but it's so easy to get sidetracked by the innumerable small projects that beckon to you as your students' arrival gets closer (alphabetizing library books, picking staples out of the bulletin boards, putting decorative labels on mailboxes) that you may wind up leaving major projects to the last minute. My favorite way of managing the urge to attend to small details right away is to write down those little projects right on the board, so there's no paper to lose. Keeping a running list in a clearly visible place assures me I won't forget, and allows me to focus on the bigger picture.

Six Principles for Room Design

There's no right way to build a classroom. However, I encourage you to take the time to design a classroom that is not only appealing and functional, but also aligned with your teaching style. Take the following ideas into consideration as you make choices.

1. **The way you arrange your classroom sends messages to your students about your values and expectations, and reflects your style as a teacher.**

A thriving classroom depends on both strong, effective leadership on the part of the teacher and a culture of shared responsibility among the students. The arrangement of students' desks or tables, the presence and design of a meeting area, the position of a teacher's workspace, and the accessibility of everyday supplies say a lot about the level of trust and the empowerment of students in a classroom.

When the arrangement of a classroom is aligned with the culture of those who use the classroom, it stays organized. As you examine the classroom layouts illustrated on pages 67–74, consider what the different designs communicate about the values and priorities of the teacher and how each design encourages teachers and students to interact and make use of the space.

Have you skipped ahead to this chapter? Be sure to do your curriculum planning first!

Chapter 2 provides a step-by-step approach to planning your year, as well as a special guide to the first days and weeks of school. Consider this: It's possible to stay late the night before school begins, getting the room set up just right—but trying to rack your brain for curriculum plans at the last minute will undermine your confidence and reduce the quality of your teaching. Keep in mind that teaching is the substance of your work.

Clipboards make it easy for these students to work together on the meeting area rug.

2. Learning takes place in a variety of contexts.

In the course of a school day, children may learn in a variety of ways:

- listening to you speak or read, or watching you use the board or chart paper, in a whole-group setting
- sharing with one another in a whole-group setting, and perhaps watching one another use the board or chart paper
- working in small groups (with or without a teacher)
- working in partnerships
- working individually

Ideally, your room will be able to accommodate each of these scenarios comfortably, without time-consuming (and chaos-causing) adjustments. Depending on the needs of the children in your class, you may need to consider some additional configurations of space, such as room for a learning specialist or paraprofessional to work side by side with a special-needs child.

3. Students need to feel a sense of ownership.

In our zeal to have things "just so" in anticipation of the first day of school, teachers can over-manage the details of the classroom. If you get too attached to your plan, you're likely to miss useful cues from students about how to make the classroom work better.

The room should tell a story about who the students are, what they are learning, and what the classroom community values. How the space is used may change as the year develops and the community evolves. As the teacher, you set the standards and create the structure, but remember to work *with* your students to refine and maintain it. Students who feel like guests in the classroom may try to please you, but they won't offer their ingenuity.

4. Structure is essential, but so is flexibility.

When you arrange furniture, materials, and your library, remember that the most successful systems make room for approximation and imperfection. Your desks and chairs will not stay perfectly aligned; your colored pencils and magic markers will get mixed up; your library will de-alphabetize itself on a daily basis; the globe balancing precariously on the radiator *will* get knocked over. If your arrangement is too rigid or precious, you will create more work for yourself. That's exactly what you're trying to avoid! Create a classroom that can be easily maintained by people who have their minds on much bigger things.

Begin with a general plan that's flexible and that accommodates a variety of personal styles. Avoid over-structuring or over-decorating the space before your students arrive, and expect to make changes when they serve the interests of the community.

5. Build in opportunities for change.

A new semester or the completion of a major curriculum unit are excellent opportunities for making changes. A seating change can reinvigorate a classroom that's sagging in midwinter or suffering from chronic social tensions. Reorganizing the library as a class can create renewed enthusiasm for the books in your room or give students an opportunity to discover a new kind of literature, such as nonfiction or poetry, that you'll soon be exploring as a class.

6. Learn to let it go.

Why do teachers keep everything? Perhaps it is because we see learning potential in every map, measuring cup, ball of yarn, or bag of potting soil that comes our way, or perhaps it is the legacy of being underfunded. However, if our closets and cabinets are full of things we *might* use, there's no room to fit in what we *do* use. Materials that should be put away wind up floating around the classroom, and then get lost or damaged because they weren't properly stored.

If you have inherited a classroom full of someone else's hoarded stuff or have been using the same classroom for a number of years, read Clearing Out and Paring Down on pages 78–79.

Work with your students to sort and categorize the books in your classroom library.

Five Classrooms, Five Approaches

Because classrooms vary enormously in size, shape, furniture type, storage capacity, and teaching and display tools, there is no blueprint that comes close to working for everyone. Instead, seek some inspiration from the following range of floor plans. Note the classroom size, seating capacity, and special features of each plan, and "read" the plans for indicators about each teacher's values and working style. I've included my own ideas at the end of the descriptions that follow each design.

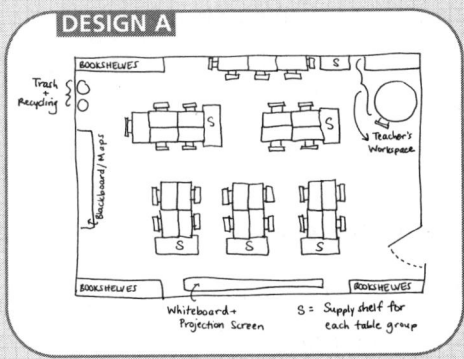

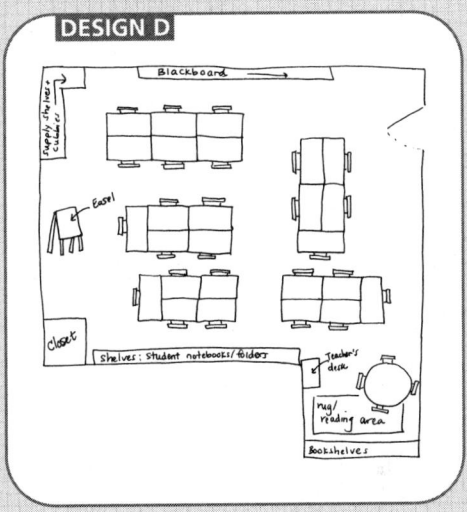

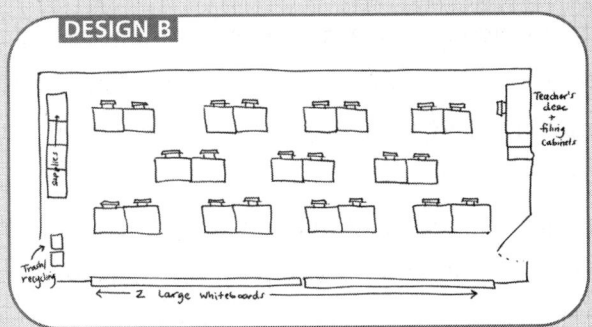

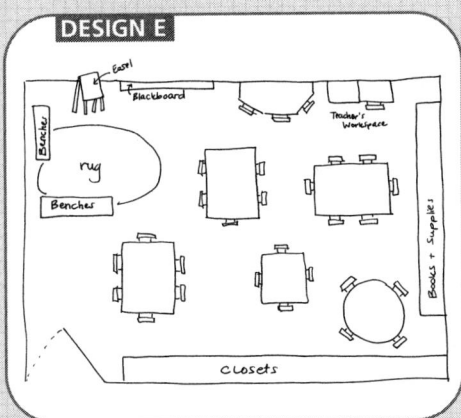

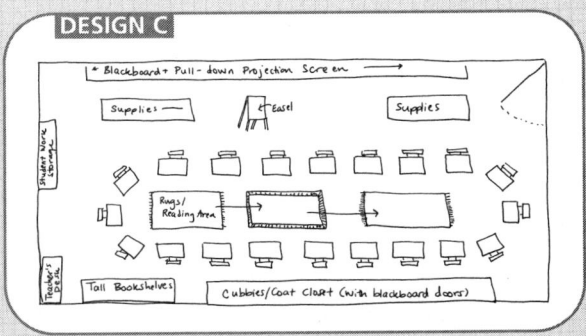

CHAPTER 3: Designing a Classroom That Will Stay Organized **67**

IDEAS YOU CAN USE:

DESIGN A

The two teachers who team-teach in this room have given each cluster of desks its own supply shelf to try to cut down on foot traffic during transitions. Each cluster's shelf contains the folders and notebooks for the students in that group, plus paper, writing utensils, glue sticks, paintbrushes, and so on.

Two of the four walls have either a blackboard or whiteboard, a feature the teachers appreciate for two reasons: First, they don't need to erase work from one activity before beginning another, and second, their students respond well to the change in perspective when beginning a new lesson.

Classroom Design Notes

The success of this setup depends on children working well within their groups. There is only one alternative workspace (the three desks along the wall) in which it is possible to work without facing another student. If they are all used regularly, the blackboards and whiteboards may create a nice sense of equality and balance in the room, since there is no permanent front or back of the room. The local supply shelves give each table a self-sufficient feel and eliminate the need for shelving around the perimeter of the room.

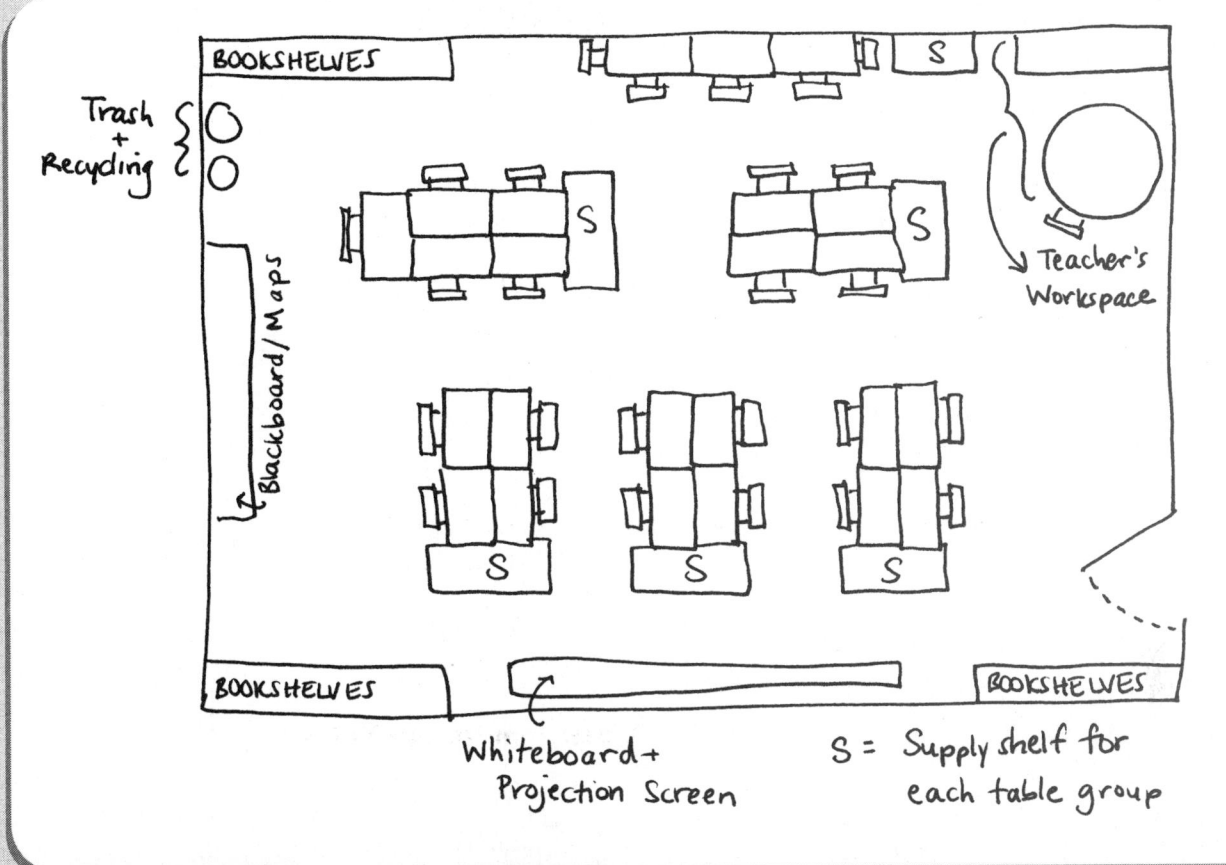

PROS:

- Alternative black/whiteboard spaces create flexible, rotating "front" of the room.
- Local supply shelves ease transitions.
- Chairs are placed in such a way that they are unlikely to back into one another.
- One private space for a small group to work.
- Workspace accommodates two teachers.

CONS:

- No space for a whole-group meeting.
- Table groupings of four to five students may be overwhelming or distracting to some learners.
- Some students will have to turn around in their seats to see the boards or the screen.

DESIGN B

This teacher, who always clustered desks in previous years, says she's trying the "one-room schoolhouse" style of pairing desks and orienting them all in one direction. She is happy with the arrangement, which "works because it's simple." In the previous year, she had whiteboards centered on two walls. For the new arrangement, she had the whiteboards moved so they are side by side, forming a giant board along one wall.

Classroom Design Notes

The arrangement of this classroom gives it a formal, presentational feel. The arrangement is most conducive to individual or partnered work. The teacher may choose to allow students to change seats in order to vary partnerships.

PROS:

- The arrangement creates a sense of structure and minimizes potential social distractions.
- Every child can easily see the whiteboard.
- The supply shelf can be accessed without disrupting work at any of the desks.

CONS:

- The uniform orientation of desks creates a definitive front and back of the room. Unless desks are rotated, this situation may encourage participation from some students while inhibiting others.
- Students cannot see one another's faces.
- The teacher may find herself "on stage" most of the time, in the same spot.
- Desks and chairs will have to be moved in order to accommodate small-group work.
- Depending upon the social reality of a classroom, it can be very difficult to pair everyone up. Sometimes a group of three or four can ease tensions or provide balance.

DESIGN C

In this long, narrow classroom, each of the 20 students sits at his or her own desk, and the desks form a long oval. Children who prefer to read on the floor do so on the three rugs arranged at the center of the oval.

The teacher who designed this room says that early in the year he experimented with clustering the desks into twos, threes, and fours around the perimeter of the oval, but separating them completely seemed to be more successful for his current group.

Classroom Design Notes

This classroom prioritizes the whole-group experience. There are no alternative workspaces for individuals or small groups (with the exception of the center of the oval, which is likely to be fairly noisy when others are working at their desks). It's probable that this design requires constant straightening of desks as they are likely to get bumped and moved frequently as students move about the room. Students who are clumsy or physically impulsive may struggle to navigate this classroom without disrupting it.

PROS:

- Students can see and hear one another well during whole-class discussions and activities.
- Rug "reading area" is relaxed and cozy.

CONS:

- Oval arrangement without opening requires that some students will have to turn around in their seats in order to see the board or easel.
- Desks and/or chairs will have to be moved in order to facilitate partnered work at desks.
- Supply access may be difficult for children on the other side of the oval.
- Teacher's workspace faces the wall and may be hard to get to.

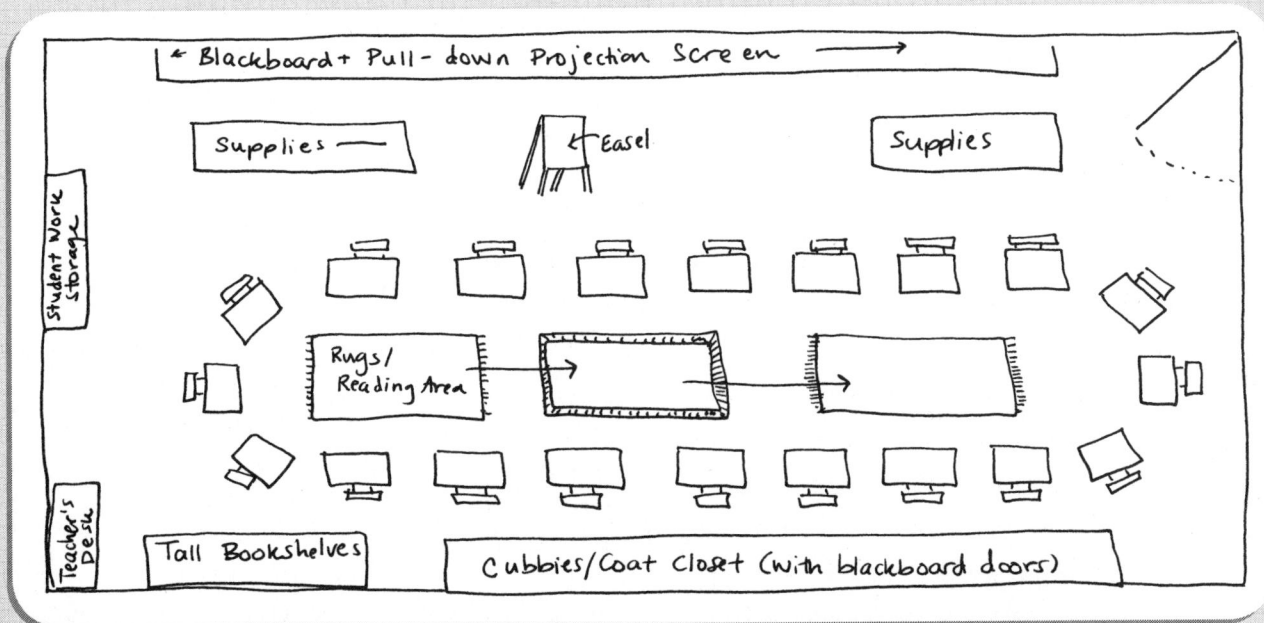

► IDEAS YOU CAN USE:

DESIGN D

The small, square space off one end of this rectangular room was originally intended to be a teacher's office. At the suggestion of her students, however, the teacher turned this part of the classroom into a quiet area for small-group work and reading.

The desks these students use do not have storage underneath. All notebooks and folders are kept in magazine racks on a long shelf along one wall. This teacher prefers such a setup—there are no messy desks to clean out, and both she and her students can access their work easily.

Classroom Design Notes

The cozy "quiet area"—and the presence of the teacher's desk in that space—communicate both a trust in students and an expectation that they behave responsibly. Although the classroom functions well when children are focused on the work at their desks, the teacher often finds she's not sure where to stand or write when addressing the whole group.

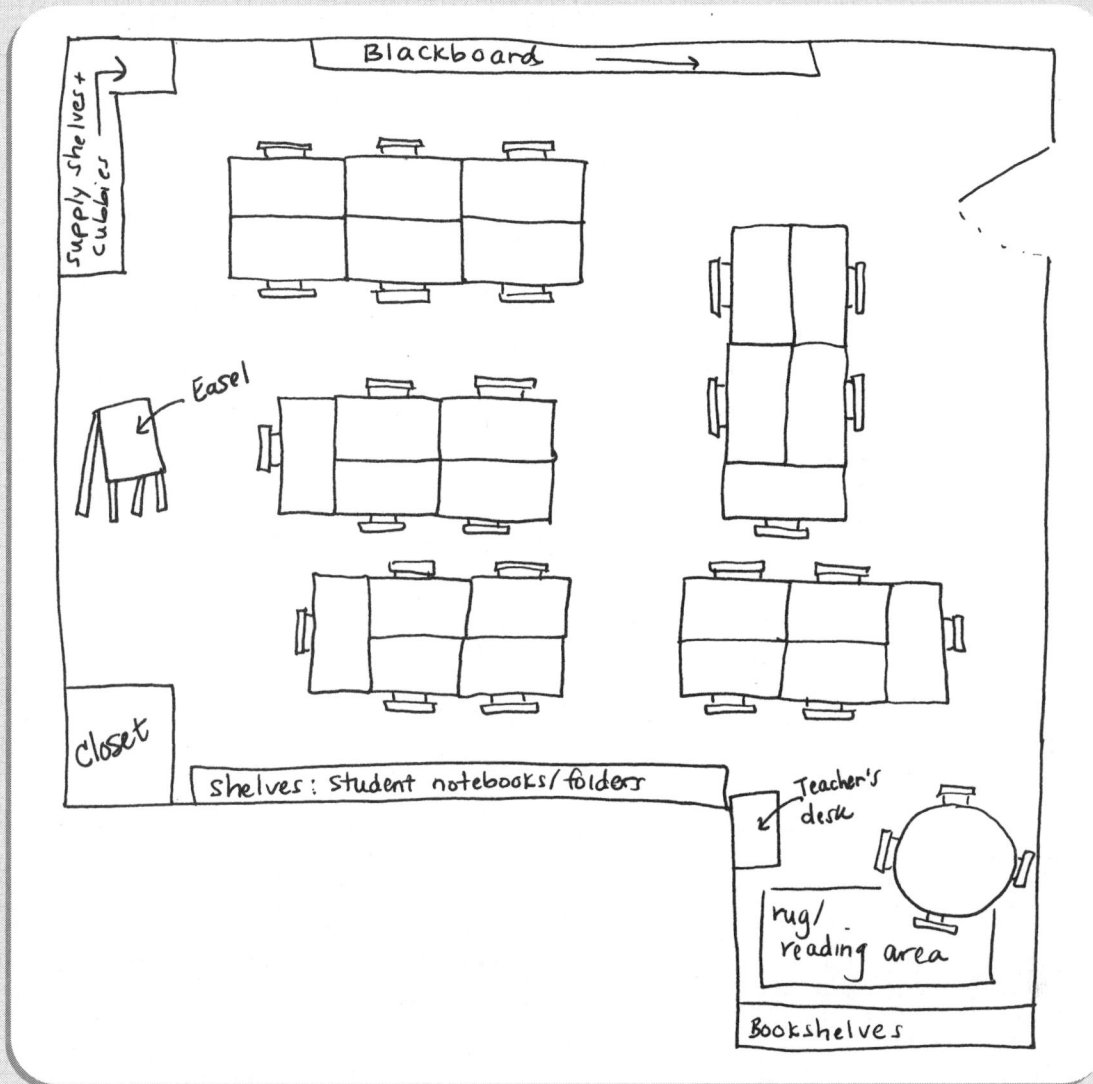

PROS:

- Supply shelves and cabinets are separate from the shelves where students keep their folders and notebooks. The teacher uses this separation to ease congestion during transitions by asking half the group to gather supplies (rulers, scissors, math manipulatives) while the other half gathers personal notebooks or folders.

- "Quiet area" table is visible from main classroom.

CONS:

- There is no whole-group meeting area where all students will be able to see one another's faces.

- About half the class will have to turn around in order to see the blackboard, and many students may have trouble seeing the easel.

CHAPTER 3: Designing a Classroom That Will Stay Organized   **73**

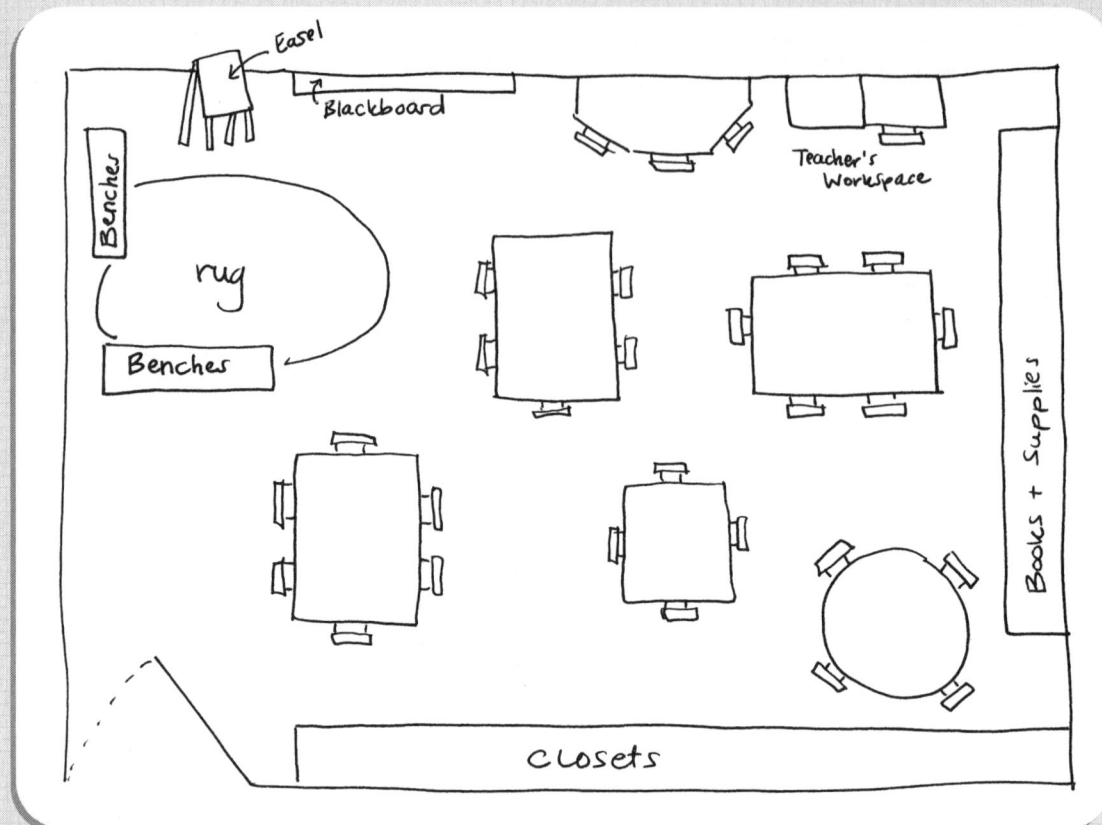

DESIGN E

Seats actually outnumber students in this room (there are 28 seats and 24 students). This teacher prefers to keep table groups fluid and flexible, grouping students (or asking them to group themselves) according to the requirements and priorities of each assignment.

Classroom Design Notes

The use of tables instead of desks creates a relaxed, clean, and flexible feel, and also makes it necessary for supplies to be stored communally. This classroom's design is most geared toward small-group work.

PROS:

- The meeting area offers both benches and seats on the floor/rug.
- Seating is relaxed and flexible.
- Large tables offer a large, smooth surface conducive to small-group work.
- Supply shelf is very long, allowing for many students to access it at once without crowding.

CONS:

- Both the blackboard and easel may be difficult to see from at least three of the six tables.
- Some students, especially young ones, may appreciate the security of an assigned seat; this arrangement may be confusing or anxiety-producing for them.
- The extra seats in this room may create traffic flow problems if students are not in the habit of pushing in their chairs.

Create Your Room

Having examined the sample classrooms, you're probably eager to begin arranging your room. However, if you are a new teacher or are teaching in a new school, it's important to know the answers to the following questions before you begin moving furniture. These questions will require a little research and thinking, but no writing.

Guiding Questions

- Do you have a choice about whether to use individual desks, grouped desks, or tables?

- Are you limited to the furniture currently in your room? Are you able to swap furniture with other teachers, or even order new furniture?

- Are there any features your room is expected to have—for example, a word wall or a meeting area?

- Is your class size likely to change during the course of the year?

- If there are other classrooms at your grade level, how are they set up?

Be clear about the way you wish to use the room as a teacher. Ask yourself the following:

- Do you expect to circulate as children work, or to stay in one place as they come to you?

- If you have a meeting area, will you sit on a chair? Will your students sit on chairs or benches, or on the floor?

- When you need to address or interact with the whole group, where would you prefer to be?

- Are there places where you can work with small groups or individuals without disturbing others?

- Where will you work when children are not in the room? Do you need a desk or other permanent "home" for your work, or a portable system you can unpack to use on students' desks or tables when they're out of the room?

Once you have read through the considerations and answered the guiding questions about classroom setup, make several copies of the grid on page 77 to sketch out a couple of alternative floor plans before you move any furniture.

Refining Your Design

When you're happy with your arrangement, read this final consideration, and make adjustments to your room design as necessary:

Children use space differently than adults. Children "read" space differently than you do. What's uncomfortable and confining to you may look cozy to a child; what's distracting to you may be soothing or focusing to him or her. The most effective way to address this issue is to make sure there are a variety of workplaces available in your classroom, including:

- an individual desk or small table that feels private.
- seats from which it's possible to look out of the windows.
- seats close to the board or chart-paper easel.
- open spaces to work on the floor.
- reading and writing "nooks" that shut out distracting sights and sounds.

! **Hold off on thinking through decisions about storing materials until later in the chapter. There's more to consider here than it may seem; see pages 80–88 for more details.**

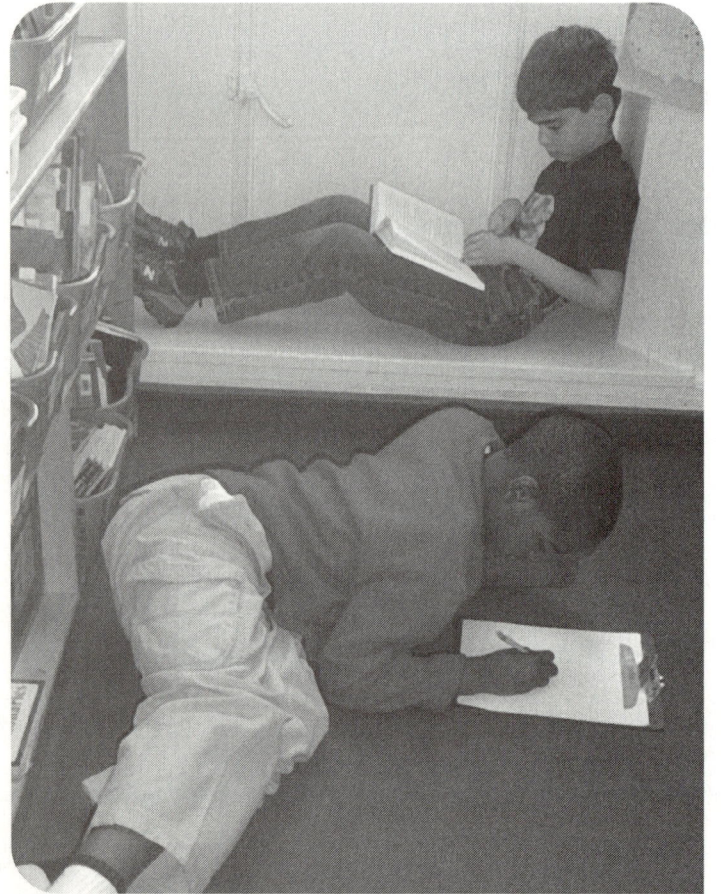

Cozy reading and writing spots help students focus.

76   Your Best Year Yet!: A Guide to Purposeful Planning & Effective Classroom Organization

Classroom Design Grid

Start by sketching your room's basic shape, and sketching any permanent features (like radiators) that take up space. Also note the location of windows and doors, including closet doors. When you add a door, draw an arc to indicate the space it will need to open comfortably.

RESOURCE PAGES

Clearing Out and Paring Down

Moving into a room long occupied by another teacher? Overhauling your own room? Begin by eliminating clutter and creating storage. Open your closet and cabinet doors, desk drawers, and filing cabinets, and use the questions below to help you decide what to keep. Then devote at least a couple of hours to throwing things out.

- Are the materials in question curriculum related? Are they current? If you find materials that are no longer relevant or current, see if your school librarian wants them, or offer them to other teachers. Otherwise, get rid of them.

- Are there art supplies—paint, clay, markers, paper—that have deteriorated over time? There's no reason to keep them. Recycle what you can.

- Are there books, textbooks, posters, or teaching materials so old that they may contain inaccurate or even offensive information? Unless you think you may be able to use a sample to teach a lesson about change over time or inclusion, get rid of them.

- Is ancient student work stored in your classroom? Try to distinguish between the kind of work that may be precious to someone—a painting or project a child spent lots of time on—and the forgettable kind (a page of long-division practice). If you discover something wonderful…

  - track down the child who made it and see if he or she wants it.
  - see if the teacher who last used your room wants to keep it.
  - find out if the staff would enjoy framing it and hanging it in the office or teachers' lounge.
  - frame it and take it home.
  - throw it out anyway; in all likelihood, it has been long forgotten.

! **Have quality materials to donate?** Check out www.iLoveSchools.com, a nationwide, Internet-based "matchmaking service" for teachers who need supplies and those who have supplies to donate. Get your students involved in a very worthwhile service project: They can help choose, sort, label, and package extra supplies for students who need them!

- Have teacher-made curriculum materials been left in your room? If you cannot imagine yourself using them, see if you can find out if the teacher who made them wants them back. Quite possibly, he or she knew they were not useful, but couldn't bear to destroy them. If the old teacher doesn't want them back, your principal and librarian show no interest, and your school has no place to archive them, just throw them out.

- Do you have too much of something useful—snap cubes, thermometers, gallon jugs of paint? Find out whether these things could be shared or donated to a school with fewer resources.

Avoid recreating the hassle next year by keeping your own hoarding to a minimum. If you're unsure about keeping something, ask yourself, "When I find this next year, will I still want it?"

Finally, if you're attempting to clear out and pare down during the school year, remember to take advantage of your students' enthusiasm for this kind of project. Get them involved!

Organizing Classroom Materials

Imagine a classroom in which materials are easily accessed and returned after use, students conserve paper and markers, no empty glue sticks or staplers remain on the shelves, and little is wasted. It *is* possible—but it takes some focused planning. Simple answers to these Guiding Questions will help you head off annoying, persistent problems with material use and storage all year long.

Guiding Questions

- Are consumable materials (paper, pencils and pens, erasers, paint, markers and colored pencils, notebooks and folders, chart paper) provided by the school? Are you responsible for ordering them, or should you pick up your share from a common supply area?

  _____

- Are you responsible for purchasing any materials yourself?

  _____

- Do teachers in your school ask families to bring in supplies?

  _____

- Which nonconsumable teaching materials (math manipulatives, scissors, paintbrushes) or equipment (globe, overhead projector, VCR, whiteboard easel) stay full-time in your classroom, and which are shared or borrowed?

  _____

  _____

  _____

  _____

Types of Storage

In all likelihood, you have a variety of storage spaces in your room, ranging from shelves and cubbies to filing cabinets and closets. The key to making the most of the storage you have is to carefully consider who needs to access which materials, and how often. You will need four types of storage in your classroom.

- **Daily Student Access:** Those materials easily accessed and maintained by any of the students in your room. Items in this category will likely include pens and pencils, several different kinds of paper, transparent tape, scissors, glue sticks, and so on—any items your students will need frequently and can use without supervision.

- **Daily Teacher Access:** Those materials that may not be accessible to students but can be easily accessed and maintained by any teacher who uses your room. These materials include specialty papers, the paper cutter, the hot-glue gun, and other materials that require supervision, as well as records that are not intended for students (or their parents) to see without consulting with you.

- **Occasional Use:** Items that may be stored in a place requiring minor effort for a teacher to access. For instance, if you use graduated cylinders for a particular science project but don't need them out all the time, they don't need to take up valuable easy-access space.

- **Long-Term Storage:** Items, such as memorabilia, materials for a once-a-year event, or curriculum materials that won't be used this year but are likely to be used in the future. These items should be boxed, labeled, and stored. If you need to climb on a chair or ask for a little help to get to it, you'll only have to do it once.

Three Steps to Arranging Materials So They'll Stay Organized

Many of the materials on the list on pages 83–84 should be stored in two places—in areas designated for daily student access *and* daily teacher access. Put out only enough consumable materials (paper, pencils, markers, and so on) for one to two weeks and talk to your students about conserving classroom materials. If the supply appears to be endless, students will use materials less thoughtfully.

✋ You can assign a student to notify you when certain supplies are low, then hand a new batch to the student so he or she can do the restocking.

STEP 1 Sort your materials.

Using checkmarks, sort the items in the list that follows into the four types of storage described on page 81. Of course, there are likely to be materials you need that are not on the list (add them on the extra lines), and those that I've included that you don't really use (delete them).

Encourage conservation of classroom consumables by keeping your backup supplies out of sight or out of reach, on a high shelf behind a curtain.

Materials Sorting Chart

Materials	Daily Student Access	Daily Teacher Access	Occasional Use	Long-Term Storage
WRITING TOOLS				
Pencils				
Pens				
Erasers				
Pencil grips				
Highlighters				
Colored pencils				
CLASSROOM TOOLS AND FASTENERS				
Staplers				
Scissors				
Three-hole punch				
Paper cutter				
Paper clips and binder clips				
Brass fasteners				
Staples				
Thumbtacks				
Velcro				
Clothespins				
String				
Yarn				
Twine				
Binder rings				

Materials	Daily Student Access	Daily Teacher Access	Occasional Access	Long-Term Storage
ART SUPPLIES				
Markers				
Permanent markers				
Crayons/oil pastels				
Tempera paint				
Watercolors				
Brushes				
Cups/muffin tins/palettes				
Newspaper				
Drop cloths				
Smocks and aprons				
PAPER				
Plain white paper (new)				
Plain white paper (recycled)				
Lined writing pads				
Three-hole-punched lined paper				
Graph paper				
Construction paper				
SPECIAL PAPER				
Index cards				
Flash cards				
Craft paper				
Mural paper				
Contact paper				
Chart paper				
MISCELLANEOUS				
Digital camera				
Fabric				

STEP 2 Assess your storage situation.

Now make a list of all the available storage in your room. Identify all closets, cubbies, sets of shelves, and drawers not reserved for personal use by students or teachers. Determine—based on the location, height, and level of accessibility of each space—into which category each should fall.

Daily Student Access	Daily Teacher Access	Occasional Use	Long-Term Storage

STEP 3 Stock the shelves.

Now put materials away. Stow long-term storage and occasional-use items first, getting them out of the way; then take your time with those materials that will be accessed daily, choosing user-friendly containers. Consider labeling cabinets and file drawers with lists of their contents. Doing so will help you stick to your system, and it will also aid substitutes or other teachers who may need to use your room.

The key to keeping materials under control is being realistic about the way students will put them away. In all likelihood, you will have some students with a meticulous attitude toward everything they do—so when it's their turn to put materials away, the staplers will be perfectly aligned and the glue sticks will be stacked in a pyramid. But of course you will also have students who will toss everything back onto the shelf so offhandedly that you'll be lucky if nothing is damaged. Therefore, your system must accommodate either scenario.

Containers do the trick. A clearly labeled container, regardless of the condition of its contents, will keep the shelf looking neat. Labeling the container's "home" on the shelf (I label index cards and use contact paper to stick them to the bottoms of shelves) will also keep materials where you and your students expect to find them.

Use containers in a clutter-prone spot.

✋ Plastic baskets are ubiquitous, and you can find plenty of them at any dollar store. You can also find beautiful baskets made of wood or natural fibers at flea markets or house sales. In addition, you can reuse many common household materials, such as those listed below. Send home a notice early in the year with specific requests. Some students might enjoy decorating these items with drawings, contact paper or wallpaper samples during free time. Following are some low-cost container ideas:

- empty plastic berry boxes (great for holding small scissors upright)
- milk jugs, washed and cut to make buckets with handles (these can hold water for painting projects)
- egg cartons (great for storing beads, magnets, marbles, classroom coins, and other small odds and ends)
- milk crates
- cigar boxes
- large coffee cans (terrific for holding paintbrushes)
- old postal crates (perfect for holding big items, like smocks)
- sturdy takeout containers with lids

If you have limited shelf space, consider one of these options:

- Store small items in zippered plastic freezer bags and clip them to a clothesline pinned to the wall.
- Check the hardware store for a miniature plastic chest designed for sorting small bits of hardware (screws, drill bits, etc.) and use it for classroom items—small sticky notes, paper clips, and so on.
- Mount a sturdy wire grid, such as those intended for hanging pots and pans, on the wall. Use "s" hooks and binder rings to hang any basket with a handle (or open wire-mesh surface) on the grid.

Make it easy for your students to take care of the room.

✋ If you want students to use bookmarks instead of dog-earing pages, hang a pocket of bookmarks beside your library shelves. Place baskets for reusable pieces of paper near the unused paper, so students can make the best choices easily. When markers dry out, discard them but keep their tops in a separate basket, right alongside the other markers; when tops disappear from working markers, students can take responsibility for replacing them.

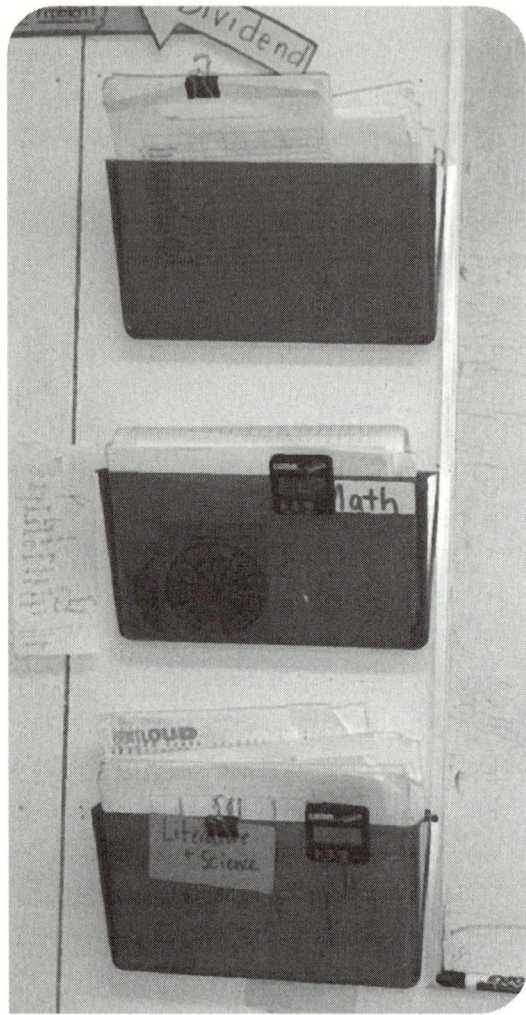

Use wall space to organize paper.

- Consolidate paper into a vertical organizer—stacking trays or wall-mounted pockets from an office supply store are very useful. Tape a single sheet of each paper type onto the bottom of its tray to help with restocking.

Creating Materials Kits

One alternative to storing materials for the whole class in a common space is to create kits for use by small groups or by students working individually, but in the same general area. Each kit, stored in a large, stackable container (such as a milk crate), contains basic classroom materials in labeled, lidded containers. The crate and all of its containers and contents should be clearly labeled with a number, letter, or symbol.

When beginning an activity or project, students simply take their crates to their work areas. If necessary, teachers can distribute additional or specialty materials that are not generally stored in the crates. Students in each group are responsible for restocking used materials at the end of their work session, so the kits are always ready to go.

Making Students Your Allies in Maintaining the Classroom

Keeping your classroom in order requires your commitment to *truly* sharing the space with your students. That means no sneaking around and "fixing" what they leave unfinished or messy. The experience of not finding what you need when you need it ("Hey! What happened to the staplers? How come there's no more construction paper?") supports learning. If students don't care for their space, yet it's magically stocked and organized each day, they won't learn how or why to care for it. Here are some tips to involve students in the care and maintenance of the room:

- **Involve students in making decisions about the changes that happen in the classroom throughout the year** (wall displays, seat changes, etc.). They don't always get the final say, but they know their ideas have been taken into account. These changes can create new social opportunities or address social problems, cheer up students and teachers alike when the class feels dull and tired, and foster an interest in the aesthetic quality of the classroom.

- **Check that classroom displays are current and reflect *everyone's* contributions.** Including everyone's work on the walls helps students feel a sense of pride in and ownership of their classroom. Not only is this good teaching practice when it comes to supporting and motivating students, but it's also a way to help students care about how the classroom looks and functions.

Make a How-To Binder

Whenever you teach your students a new protocol or routine they're likely to use often—for instance, having a writing conference with a peer, solving a multi-step math problem, using editing symbols, writing in the Class Journal, cleaning out the hamster cage—write down the steps, title the page, and add it to a How-To binder. When students ask for reminders, direct them to the binder.

Showcase everyone's work.

- **Make sure students understand how the classroom works and that they have a key role to play in helping it to work well.**

Take the time early in the year to demonstrate to students how to put new staples in the stapler, reload the tape dispensers, tap a stack of paper on a table to align all the pages, and so on (this can be done in 20 or 30 seconds at the beginning of a morning meeting). Model conservation of classroom materials: Reuse the backs of chart-paper pages whenever possible; specify whether a particular activity *requires* a new sheet of paper or whether it's fine to use the back of another. Make sure each student's responsibilities are real: If you assign a student to water plants and he doesn't do it, draw his—and the class's—attention to the thirsty plants, rather than just watering them yourself.

Setting Up for Easy Maintenance

To ensure the time you invest in setting up your room is well spent, and that you don't find yourself overhauling the room in December or dogged by annoyances all year long, keep the following pointers in mind as you set up your classroom.

- **Assess your storage situation thoughtfully, and make purposeful decisions about who will need access to which materials, and how often.**

- **Only put out what is likely to be used in the next one to two weeks.**

- **Keep materials where they're used.**

- **If you want your students to use recycled materials whenever possible (especially paper), make these more accessible than the new materials.**

- **Make choices that support your students' investment in the classroom.**

Putting Students to Work: Classroom Jobs

There are many ways children can help maintain the classroom. Some classroom jobs have been highlighted in this book; depending on the needs of your particular classroom, you may be able to come up with many others. Note that some jobs are done daily, and some weekly; still others are "on call" types of jobs. Remember that in order to be successful contributors, students will need explicit instruction and practice early in the year.

Some jobs need to be done at specific times, but most are integrated right into the life of the room. There's no need to schedule a "job time" if your students' responsibilities correspond to the needs of the community. Select community jobs that appeal to third to fifth graders, such as the following:

Teacher's Helpers

- **paper handler**: passes out and/or collects class work, homework, blank paper, and so forth.
- **alphabetizer**: puts stacks of notebooks or papers in alphabetical order so record-keeping is easier and faster for the teacher
- **messenger**: delivers notes to other teachers or to the office
- **display helper**: "frames" work with construction paper; helps design displays, tack them up, and take them down

Peer Support and Leadership Roles

- **nurse buddy**: accompanies students to the nurse's office if they are sick or hurt
- **librarian**: keeps library neat, and recommends a favorite book during a morning meeting

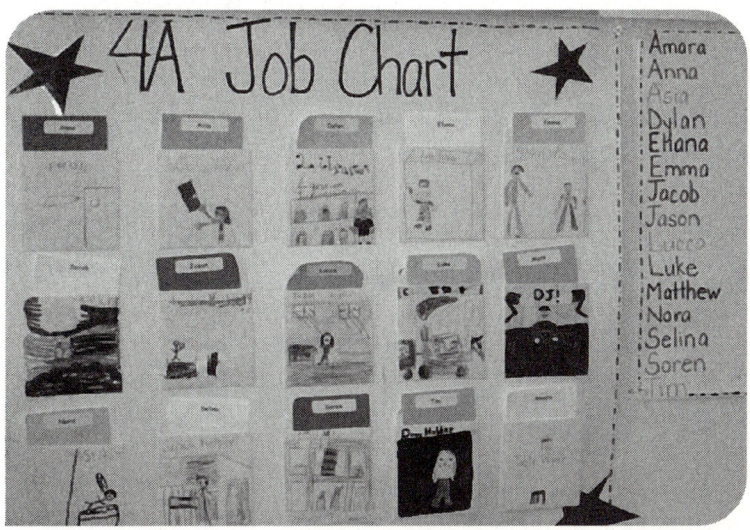

A job chart can have pockets illustrated by students.

✋ **Want to put an end to Chronic Sharpening Syndrome (oh, that screeching, grating noise!)?** Some students can't resist the urge to use the sharpener, especially when the rest of the class is hard at work and silent. Here's a solution: Put out a basket for pencils that need sharpening or an eraser cap right next to a basket of new pencils. If a student needs a new pencil, he or she can exchange it for a new one without disturbing the class. At the end of the day, the student with the pencil maintenance job can get all the pencils in good shape for the next day.

- **ambassador**: helps visitors or new students learn their way around and keeps them company at lunch and recess; explains classroom projects or displays to parents or visitors with questions
- **"special meeting" leader**: decides on a topic for the class to discuss or debate, and moderates the discussion
- **current-events reporter**: chooses, with teacher and parent approval, a news story to follow and share with the class throughout the week
- **Class Journal writer** (see page 13)

Room Maintenance Jobs

- **supply chief**: keeps supplies organized and replenishes them as necessary
- **pencil-maintenance clerk** (see tip at left)
- **sweeper**
- **spill crew**: deals calmly and efficiently with spills of math manipulatives, colored pencils, juice, paint, and so on.
- **board eraser/board washer**: cleans all boards at the end of the day
- **animal caretaker**: feeds pets and maintains cages or aquariums, with a teacher's help when necessary
- **plant caretaker**: waters and maintains plants
- **recycling chief**: ensures bins are emptied regularly and reminds students to recycle whenever possible
- **bits and pieces helper** (a perennial favorite with my students): crawls around under desks at the end of the day, collecting colored pencils, math manipulatives, paper clips, scrap paper, and so on. that have been dropped, and returns them to their rightful places

Jobs That Benefit the Greater School Community

- **guest reader**: reads to a partner in a kindergarten or first-grade classroom (see Classroom Buddies tip at right)
- **recycling expert**: teaches younger students about classroom recycling (see Classroom Buddies tip)
- **custodians and decorators**: maintain school common spaces (like the lobby or cafeteria), or decorate common spaces in preparation for holidays or special events
- **secret admirer**: writes an unsigned note of thanks and appreciation to a school worker (custodian, office worker, cafeteria worker) whose contribution the school counts on

Summary

The quiet of August or September, before school begins, can be deceiving. As the lone inhabitant of your room (and as an adult), it's easy to make design and organizational choices that suit you but can't be easily sustained by your students.

As you arrange your room, keep your attention on how it will function when the room is in motion. When you make choices about the placement of furniture and materials, think about your students—how they move through a crowded space, what they can reach, what captures and holds their attention, and what matters to them. Leave the room unfinished—for example, don't cover the walls with posters—so that students can enjoy a sense of expectation and possibility as they enter for the first time.

One of the central lessons of my year at P.S. 89 (see The Year That Inspired This Book, pages 4–7) was that the miniature society students build with their teacher provides the essential energy of a classroom. A well-stocked, beautifully organized classroom cannot impose order on a chaotic, unpredictable, or unbalanced interpersonal world. However, when both teacher and students are committed to creating a community, a little order goes a long way. Refer back to Chapter 1 for ideas about how to make classroom community happen.

Classroom Buddies

Some schools have a well-established buddy class tradition in which younger students develop special relationships with students in a higher grade. Little Red School House in Manhattan uses this idea beautifully: Buddy classes establish relationships by reading together once a week and teaming up for art projects. Then, as the year progresses, they join together to sing in musical assemblies or for a day of outdoor games and picnicking in Central Park.

Younger children are thrilled by their personal connections to the older ones, and older students take great pride in their special teaching responsibilities. If your school doesn't have a buddy class system, suggest it to an administrator. You may also be able to make arrangements directly with another teacher.

CHAPTER 4

Taming All That Paper:
Classwork, Homework, Record-Keeping, and Reporting Student Progress

Teachers handle a lot of paper. We have piles of pages that need to be copied, distributed, checked, sorted, returned for changes, sent home, and filed. We have class work and homework, individual work and group work. Students cart around some of their work in their backpacks and leave some of it in the classroom, and frequently they use separate folders or notebooks for each content area.

Once a teacher gets just a little bit behind, the backlog seems to grow exponentially. The paper we need is hard to find, and the paper we no longer need has no clear place to go. In my first years of teaching I often felt so overwhelmed by the amount of work I needed to do, I filed whole, unsorted piles of work right in the recycling bucket. But there are ways to avoid getting overwhelmed and taking such extreme measures.

This chapter builds on the system outlined in Chapter 2 for controlling the paperwork involved in planning and on the ways to achieve efficient organization of materials described in Chapter 3. Here we focus on the creation of a clutter-free system for student-generated paperwork and for record-keeping.

Preventing Paper Clutter

The first step in eliminating paper clutter is to reduce the amount of paper you use in the first place. Here are some ideas for how to accomplish that goal:

✻ **Decide ahead of time whether you need paper at all for certain projects.** Sometimes the writing and figuring involved in an assignment or project are essential to keep and review—and sometimes they're not. When the note taking, figuring, sorting, or sketching your students will do is the type that doesn't need to be saved, consider a reusable surface. You can make miniature whiteboards by putting cardstock or white shirt cardboard through a laminating machine, and have your students use them with black dry-erase pens and clean rags or baby socks for erasing.

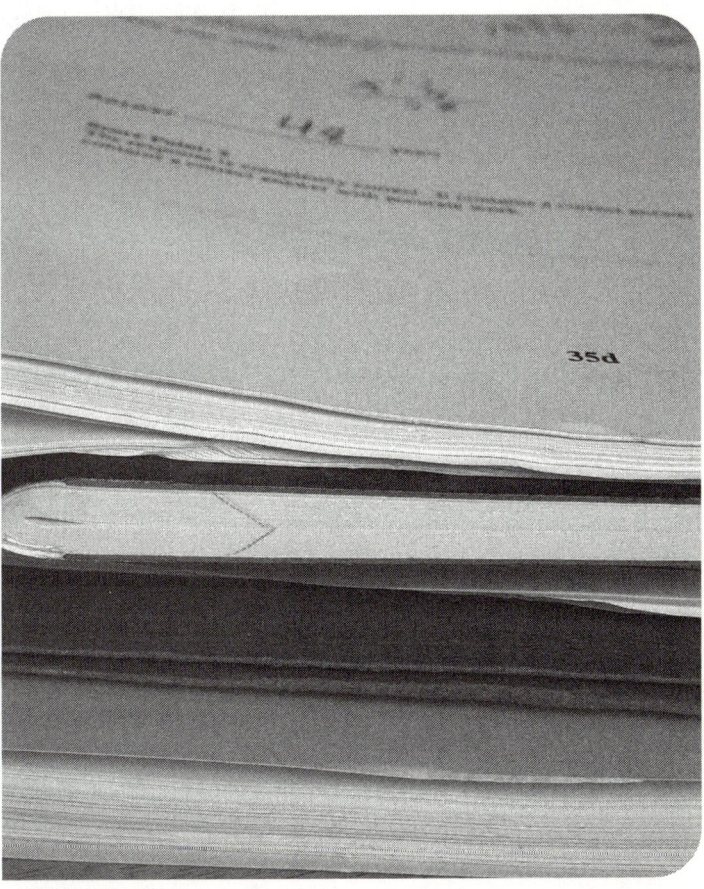

Avoid the bottomless pile.

> **!** Even if you reduce the amount of paper used in your classroom, there will still be plenty to handle. These four simple strategies will help you create an efficient system for doing so:
>
> - Reduce the number of categories you sort paper into.
> - Use as little *loose* paper as possible.
> - Every stack of paper should be in alphabetical and/or chronological order.
> - Share responsibility for sorting, distributing, collecting, and filing paper with your students.

✱ **Have students work in partnerships and small groups more frequently.** Research supports the value of talk in learning. Find opportunities for students to work together on projects, sharing ideas as well as paper as they work. When they are finished, the group can hand in a single page representing their collaborative efforts.

✱ **Work together.** Use the board, a chart pad, or an overhead projector to work on a skill or an idea as a class, so students don't need to work on individual sheets of paper.

✱ **Make double-sided copies whenever you can.** When you create forms for your own or your students' use—library checkout forms, class lists, homework forms—photocopy them on both sides of a page. Forms designed for lists can often be duplicated several times on each side of a page.

✱ **Use the back!** A sheet of instructions, a score sheet from a math game, or a completed checklist is a learning tool, not an end in itself. It may not be useful enough to keep, but it's wasteful to throw it out. Why not use the other side for similar tasks? Keep a basket for paper that can be reused—and make it more accessible than the brand-new paper.

✱ **Keep more than one kind of scrap paper** (full-size, half-size, and quarter-size), each in its own basket. Reuse whatever single-sided pages you can, and regularly cut non-confidential memos, printing and photocopying mistakes, and so on, into halves or quarters with a paper cutter to restock the baskets. When your class needs paper for keeping score for a math game, writing a spelling list, or making a quick sketch, provide them with the smallest size that will do the job.

✱ **Customize a Planbook** so it has plenty of room for your own notes, reminders, and reference lists—groupings, phone numbers, to-dos—allowing you to avoid chasing scraps and sticky notes all over the room. (See Customizing a Planbook, page 45.)

Managing the Paper You Need

Don't be caught off-guard by your school's expectations for record-keeping and reporting. Before setting up a system for managing paper in your room, find answers to the following questions.

Guiding Questions

Does your school require students to have any particular tools, such as a writer's notebook, a literature journal, or a math log? If so, are you free to decide on the format of these tools?

_____

_____

_____

_____

Are you expected to send work home frequently to families, or store it for periods of time for assessment purposes?

_____

_____

_____

_____

Will you use a portfolio system for collecting work? Does it have a prescribed structure? Who will see it?

_____

_____

_____

_____

When you are clear about your school's expectations, you are ready to design a system for managing the flow of student work and keeping your records organized and current.

A System That Works

Basically, student work falls into two categories: work that is current (includes work that is in progress or needs corrections), and work that is finished (both student and teacher are satisfied). Finished work falls into two categories, also. It is either worth saving or not worth saving. Finally, work that is worth saving falls into two categories as well: work that goes home and work that stays in school. Therefore, your students need a place for current work and a place for finished work that will be archived in school. See the flow chart below.

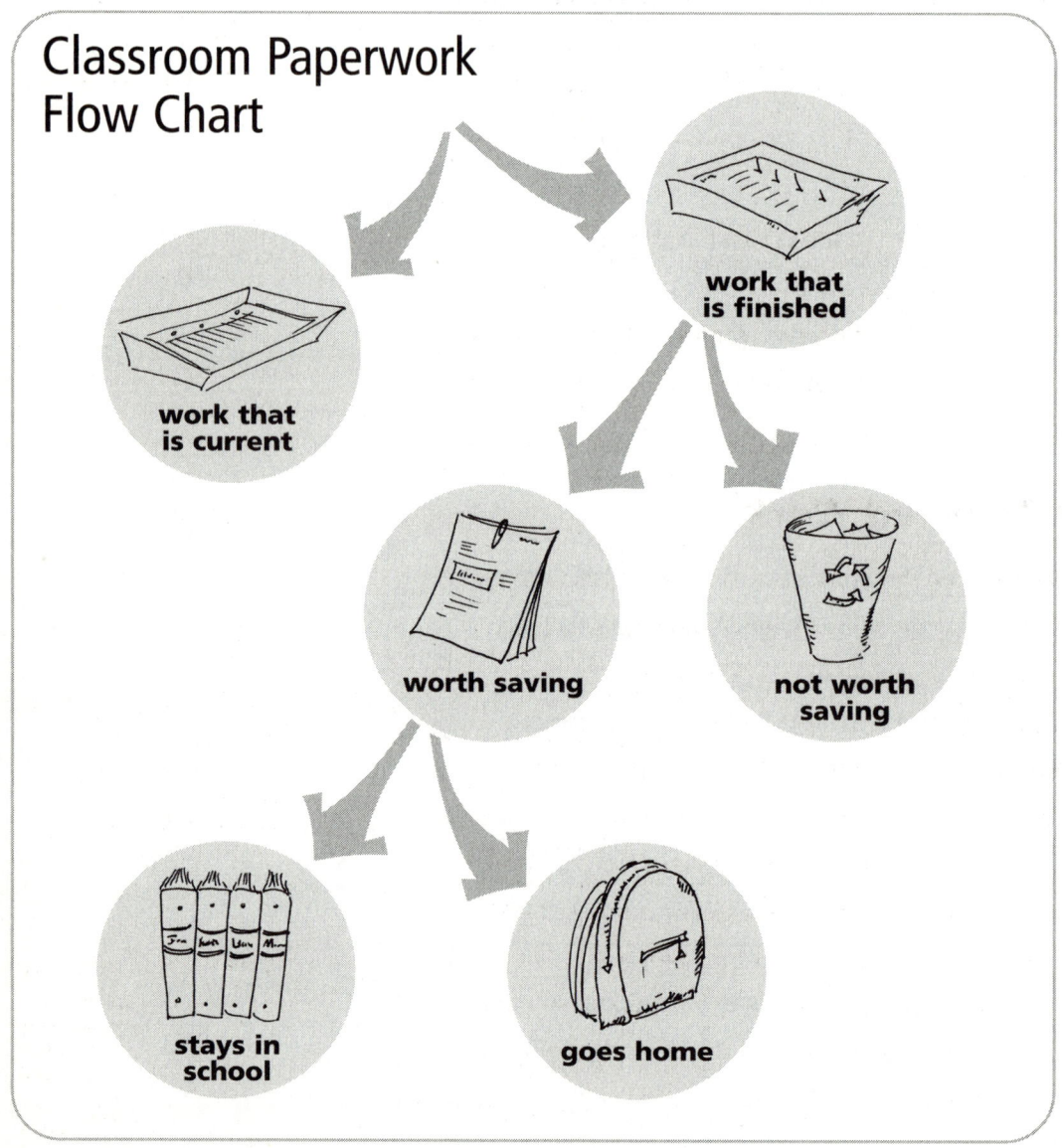

Classroom Paperwork Flow Chart

- work that is current
- work that is finished
- worth saving
- not worth saving
- stays in school
- goes home

A Place for Current Work

Many teachers prefer to use separate notebooks or folders for each subject area. At one time, I supplied my students with math journals, social studies notebooks, writer's notebooks, reading response journals, and science journals. I found, however, that while some notebooks filled up quickly, others were used infrequently and seemed unnecessary. Therefore, in recent years, my students have begun using a single folder and only two additional notebooks.

In this simplified system, the folder is called the Current Work Folder and holds all current work: class work in progress, work that needs correcting, and extensions—activities or special challenges to work on when other work is finished (see Extensions, page 100). Students label one pocket of the folder "In Progress" and the other side "Extensions." The entire collection of folders is kept in alphabetical order and divided among two or three bins or large baskets (to avoid traffic jams when children are accessing them).

In addition to the folders, students use Writer's Notebooks, which travel back and forth to school and need to remain intact (pages are not removed). They also use Reflection Journals, an assessment tool described in detail, with examples, on pages 114–116.

A Place for Archived Work

Before deciding how to store the student work that stays in school, you should be clear about what will stay in school, and why (see Deciding What Goes Home on page 103). For instance, you may intend to use a portfolio system to collect artifacts that represent each student's growth throughout the year, and use that portfolio for assessment and reporting purposes. On the other hand, you may rely primarily on tests and quizzes for your assessment data, and send most class work home when it has been completed. The size, arrangement, and organization of your archiving space will be determined by your teaching style and assessment practices.

Extensions: A Solution for Fast Finishers

"I'm done! What should I do?"

I remember clearly the day my own fourth-grade teacher became exasperated with my friend Sharon and me for repeatedly asking him this question. Having run out of ideas for extra assignments, he finally gave each of us two paper towels—one to go under each foot—and told us to race each other in the hallway without lifting our feet off the ground.

Years later, not wanting to resort to the same solution (but feeling tempted), I came up with the Extensions pocket on my students' current work folders. Whenever a student is finished with a whole-class project or activity and has no outstanding corrections or unfinished work, I refer them to their Extensions pocket.

Before the year begins and as it continues, I collect ideas for high-quality activities such as special math challenges, problem-solving activities, and crosswords and word games that I think my students would enjoy. I also reserve extra copies of certain skill-based activities: long division, for example—and reincarnate them, months later, as extensions. I make sure the instructions for all activities in the Extensions pocket are easy to understand, so students can work on them without much assistance from me.

I add them to students' folders in small batches, and often individualize them. For instance, if I notice that a particular student has trouble remembering how to make certain capital letters in cursive, I may add a few pages of practice to her Extensions pocket. A math challenge with universal appeal and utility might go to everyone.

Finally, I make sure that no one's pocket is too full, because a slow worker or a child who is struggling academically may feel bogged down or overwhelmed by a bulging folder full of things to do.

When you compile extension activities, look around for grade-appropriate books of math or language challenges that suit your style. In addition to anything you make yourself, you can photocopy a whole bunch of activities at a time and have them ready to use.

To store extension activities, use a three-ring binder with dividers labeled by content area. Write a quick note on the upper right-hand corner of each activity indicating its basic focus ("multi-step problem solving," "editing symbols," "facts vs. opinions"). This saves time when you're looking through the binder for ideas or searching for something to complement the skills you're covering in class.

You will need to decide who will access the archived work—you, your students, or both. So along with size, arrangement, and organization of archived work, it's important to consider the aspect of accessibility.

Materials

To create a binder or portfolio that holds archived work, begin with one of two tools: a multi-pocket, spiral-bound portfolio (usually each pocket is a different color) or a three-ring binder with dividers (a "file binder"). I prefer using portfolios with younger children to eliminate the hassle of three-hole-punching new additions, and the binder system with older children who will need to know how to organize and maintain binders in the middle-school years.

Either order the binders or portfolios yourself or provide parents with *very precise* descriptions of what students should bring in. The uniformity of binders or portfolios is part of what makes the system

Label binders for archived work in a consistent way so that your students can easily keep them in order.

Helping With the Room

Keep a list of "room projects" tacked to the wall, such as taking down displays, framing student work with construction paper, shining up the aquarium, decorating the cover of the Class Journal, sorting out math manipulatives, and so on. You may get to some of these tasks yourself—but sometimes you can refer students to the list rather than to their Extensions folders (see page 100).

as a whole easy to manage. Send home a notice clearly specifying the size and material of the binder or portfolio (for instance: "one-inch-thick three-ring binder, standard size, stiff covers, no closing flaps, solid colors only"). If possible, purchase a few extras so that when one or two students show up with "illegal" binders, you can replace them with approved ones and send the others home again with a polite note and a copy of your original notice.

Label the spines of the binders or portfolios with your students' names and arrange them in alphabetical order in several portable file boxes, large baskets, or sturdy magazine racks, in such a way that the bindings are facing the same way and all the names are lined up. Using a number of containers instead of just one or two cuts down on congestion when the whole class is attempting to retrieve archived work (or add to it) at the same time.

Personalizing and Organizing the Binders or Portfolios

If you wish, allow some school time early in the year for decorating the front and back covers of binders and portfolios. The spines of the binders are never decorated, and instead are labeled clearly with each student's name in the same place. This makes the process of alphabetizing or locating binders quick and easy for both you and your students.

After decorating the covers, students using binders can learn to insert labels into the dividers, and then add a divider for each content area.

When using portfolios, allow students to decorate the front and back covers. I write each student's initials on a very small piece of white electrical tape with a permanent marker, and place it over a portion of the spiral binding. Portfolio users then label each of the folders in their own handwriting—"Math," "Social Studies," and so on.

Teach your students to write the date on everything that gets archived, and to put their most recent work in front of the appropriate section in their binder or portfolio.

Deciding What Goes Home

It's not practical to keep archiving student work indefinitely. Those file binders will begin "exploding" (as students might say), a couple of months into the school year. In addition, not every piece of work a student produces is relevant or representative of his or her progress. Keeping too much student work in the room creates both storage and assessment hassles, and it makes it difficult for parents to know what's going on in school.

However, sending everything home also creates assessment dilemmas—how can you know how far your students have come if you can't remember where they started out? Beyond the work on display in your room, be on the lookout for artifacts worth keeping (or photocopying) for assessment purposes, or to illustrate a point in a parent conference.

Give your students an opportunity to reflect on their own progress. Take 15 or 20 minutes once in a while—at the end of a unit, or right before a vacation—and examine the contents of file binders or portfolios as a class. As children look through their binders, circulate and discuss with individual students what they'd like to share with their families, and why. Encourage them to look for examples of growth, not perfection ("Wow—look at the difference between those essays you wrote in the fall and the ones you're writing now!"). If a student wants to take something home that you feel should remain in school, either photocopy it or be clear with the student that the item will be "on loan" for a week or so, but must be returned to the classroom at a later date.

The System in Action

Now that all components of the system are set—you have places for current and archived work and plans for how to keep the paperwork organized—let's take a look at how to use the system effectively.

Beginning and Ending a Work Period

At the beginning of a work period, two students pass out the Current Work Folders. Anything we're currently working on—projects or assignments that are in progress—are in the In Progress pocket of the Current Work Folder. Remember that notebooks containing current work can be stored in Current Work Folders as well. Assignments can be bookmarked so teachers and students can locate them easily (see the photo on page 109).

When the work period is over, individual pages and notebooks are tucked back into the folders, the folders are collected, and perhaps alphabetized, by students assigned to do so (see the list of classroom jobs on pages 91–93), and then returned to the baskets or file boxes. You can access any student's work—or track the progress of the class as a whole—by retrieving the folder(s) you need. Because students leave their most recent projects on top, you won't have to rifle through their work to find what you're looking for. The next section shows how to use alphabetized class lists to make your recording process efficient.

(Above) Tucking notebooks into the In Progress pocket of the Current Work Folder keeps students' work organized.

(Below) Alphabetized by name, students' work folders are easy to find.

Using Class Lists With Current Work Folders

A stack of class lists can be extremely useful in a number of situations: tracking everyone's progress on a project, keeping track of who has turned in homework or permission slips, and so on.

You can add a grid to the list (see the sample below) for keeping records or taking very brief notes on each student's progress on weekly projects. In addition, you may decide to carry a list with you on a clipboard as you circulate during student work periods, so you can make notes about who seems to need extra help, and who is finished or almost finished. When you have time to look at everyone's written work closely during a prep period or after school (see Reviewing and Returning Student Assignments, pages 106–107), you can check off completed assignments or make additional notes.

Since both the Current Work Folders and the class lists are alphabetized, and since students organize their work chronologically inside their folders, you can work your way through the stack of Current Work Folders quickly and efficiently, taking notes as you go.

Student Name	Directed Essay	Division Story Problems	Animal Brochure	Lab Sheet	Letter to the Editor	Spelling Word Sort	Continents and Oceans
Anabeth	✓	✓		✓		✓	✓
Anna	✓	✓	✓	✓		✓	✓
Carlos	✓		✓		✓	✓	✓
Dana		✓	✓	✓	✓	✓	✓
Jacob	✓	✓		✓	✓	✓	✓
Jenny	✓	✓	✓	✓	✓		
Josh B.	✓		✓	✓	✓	✓	✓
Josh N.	✓	✓	✓		✓	✓	✓
Kira	✓	✓	✓	✓	✓	✓	
Lizzie	✓		✓		✓		✓
Monique	✓	✓	✓	✓	✓	✓	

Some projects or activities take one work period and that's all. Or sometimes the class meets a deadline and everyone turns in finished work at the same time. Therefore, keep a To Be Checked basket separate from the Current Work Folders. Student helpers collect the finished work, alphabetize it, and clip it together before placing it in the basket.

Reviewing and Returning Student Assignments

Students should understand that you want them to continue working on their schoolwork until you're *both* satisfied. During a prep period, at lunchtime, or at the end of the school day—whenever you have time to review assignments closely—decide who is *actually* finished, with no revisions or corrections necessary. Here are some suggestions to streamline the process.

- **Create a symbol to indicate that work is done to your satisfaction.** I use a tiny, neutral sticker on the upper right-hand corner of the page (the sticker is not a prize—it just means "finished"). Beside the sticker, I write a brief, descriptive comment on the work, such as "Your thinking is so clear!" or "Your sketch really helped me understand what you mean!" On my class list, I use a checkmark to record the completed assignment. Then I return it to the very front of the Extensions pocket. Students can take a few seconds to file it in their binders at the beginning of the next independent work period (see tip at right), before they begin working on any Extensions.

- **If you are not satisfied, make sure students understand why.** Either directly on the work or on a sticky note, write something like: "Good start! You still need to…" and return it to the front of either the student's In Progress or Extensions pocket, depending on how promptly you want the student to complete the work. Students will have two opportunities to make any necessary changes or corrections: the next time they dig into their Current Work Folders, and during independent work time.

The Homework Factor

By third grade, some children have vast amounts of homework. Quite often, that means vast amounts of paper used and photocopies made, and piles of paper for teachers to review. To minimize paper clutter, consider using a single, sturdy composition notebook for all homework assignments (children may go through several notebooks a year) and "paste-ins," which are described below.

Keep It Together: The Virtues of Using a Single Notebook for Homework

Using one notebook for all homework has distinct advantages. A single notebook provides an excellent perspective on growth over time (provided you are clear with your students about using the pages in order); it contains previous assignments and comments for reference; it stays neat and travels easily. Certain pages can be used over long periods of time for running lists, like reading logs or spelling lists. Comments on student work are easily accessible to both students and parents.

Often, homework assignments involve written instructions. Avoid using class time for students to copy problems and instructions from the board into their books. Instead, use the copy and paste

> **!** At least twice a week, and sometimes more often, my class has a half-hour period called Worktime. This is the time to catch up on unfinished work and make revisions and corrections to work I have reviewed. It's also a time I can focus on one student or small group at a time while my other students work independently and at their own pace. If a student has no unfinished work, he or she can always move to the rest of the Extensions pocket.
>
> In addition, Worktime is the time to file work that has been officially approved by me, as signaled by the little sticker in the upper right-hand corner. Students who have work to file in their portfolios or binders do so during this time, three-hole-punching their work themselves if necessary. Again, all work in portfolios and binders is filed chronologically, most recent work in front (or on top).

It's easy to add a "paste-in."

! To help students manage their homework time, tell them about the week's assignments on Monday. Students and their families will be better able to plan the week and reserve time for other facets of their lives. To discourage students from rushing through a week's worth of homework on Monday afternoon (so they can have the rest of the week "free"), hold off on distributing the details, instructions, or materials required for each assignment until the day you'd like students to begin working on it.

commands on your word-processing program to set several copies of the instructions or examples on the same page. Then photocopy enough of these pages for your class and use a paper cutter to cut the pages into sections, one for each student.

Using glue sticks, students paste the assignments into their notebooks. They do their problem solving either directly on the homework form or the notebook page so there's no loose paper to lose.

If students need to work on the assignment page (as with a page of computation practice), shrink the page on the copier and trim the copies slightly so that they are the same size as a homework notebook page. File the originals in the Artifact Binder (see Chapter 2) for that curriculum area.

Practical Additions to the Homework Notebook

It's useful to incorporate certain kinds of reference materials into the homework notebook. For instance, you may decide to have students paste in strips of cursive letters, a list of hard-to-spell curriculum-related words, or a label with the school's Web site printed on it. In my class, when we develop a process for writing essays or learn a set of symbols for editing written work, I make copies of the steps in the process and the symbols, and have children glue those into their homework notebooks.

It's easy to find special resources such as those described above if the pages are marked. I keep a big supply of medium-size self-adhesive labels in a few different colors for making page markers. Students attach one tip of a label to the top of a page they want to mark, and then carefully fold the label in half, so the sticky sides adhere and the bottom of the label is attached to the back of the same page. Then they print a name for the page ("Cursive Letters") directly on the label.

Other features to consider adding to the notebook to improve its usefulness include:

- **a communication pocket:** a library pocket, glued to the inside of the front cover to create a safe, consistent place for notes from parents.

- **a handwriting reference guide:** self-adhesive strips of print or script letters, attached to the inside of the back cover.

- **a homework-notebook marker:** a laminated bookmark (made by the student) attached with string to the cover of the notebook, for marking the beginning of a new week of homework.

A laminated bookmark marks the page of the homework assignment.

CHAPTER 4: Taming All That Paper: Classwork, Homework, Record-Keeping, and Reporting

How Single Notebooks Keep Teachers on Track

Since homework notebooks need to go home with students virtually every day, you can't wind up with stacks of uncorrected homework papers teetering on your desk. The daily deadline will keep you from procrastinating. Certainly, some days will go by that you just won't be able to get to the homework. If that happens, you can still access the backlog easily—and there are no piles of papers to sort or lose.

Students also will cheerfully relieve you from some of the more tedious tasks related to certain types of homework. If they have completed a page of long multiplication practice, for instance, they can easily correct their own work. Ask students to choose any colored pencil they like (to distinguish it from the regular pencil they must use for their homework) and mark their own work as you review the assignment as a class. As a variation, children can partner up, check their work against each other's, and rework any problems or questions on which they disagree. They can correct their work, if necessary, in colored pencil without erasing their original answers. Later, when you review their notebooks, a quick look at the number of colored pencil marks will tell you how well they understood the assignment. If there seems to be a lot, a closer look is certainly warranted; but if your teaching is effective and your assignments are appropriate, this should be the exception, not the rule.

When assignments require careful review, take the time to write descriptive comments on them. In doing so, you'll communicate to your students that you respect their efforts. In addition, they'll be able to use your comments from one week to help them refine their work the following week.

Tracking Homework Habits

To keep track of homework, use a separate stack of class lists photocopied onto a special color of paper you have designated for homework. Label the lists each week with the names of the assignments. Check off assignments done to your satisfaction and note missing or incomplete assignments. Because there are many

> **!** Whether the homework is the one-right-answer kind or the sort that you need to read thoroughly and respond to, use the same "finished" symbol or sticker that you use for work done in class. For satisfactorily completed work, the accompanying comment may be a quick "Great job!" or a more extensive, descriptive response. On the other hand, an assignment may receive no "finished" mark, and instead have clear instructions for finishing or redoing incomplete work. That work can happen at home or during independent work time, depending on your needs and priorities on a given day.

variables in a student's home life that may affect why work may not get done on time, make decisions on a case-by-case basis about how to deal with the missing work (e.g., reassign it as homework, ask a child to do it at independent work time or during recess, or just let it go). In any case, the raw data provided by your weekly class lists will help you discuss with a student's family any chronic problem.

Sending Notebooks (and Other Items) Home

A set of mailboxes like those used in offices (you probably have one in your main office or faculty lounge) is a terrific tool for distributing and/or collecting paper. You can label the mailboxes in alphabetical order; anything you or a student collects from them will be alphabetized too, effortlessly. For instance, after you've checked the homework notebooks for the day, you can bring them (in an alphabetized stack) to the mailboxes and redistribute them. Any notices that arrive in your room during the day can be added to the mailboxes as well. Teach students to empty their mailboxes before they leave the room at the end of the day. An additional advantage of mailboxes is that they allow you to set aside notices and homework in a place where absent students can retrieve them later, independently.

Mailboxes are a personalized way to stay organized.

Truly Useful Assessment

Make assessment part of your work every day, rather than saving it up for certain times during the year. It's helpful to think of assessment as a resource for the student, his or her parents, and you as the teacher. High-quality assessment is not an end in itself; instead, it should inform your curriculum and allow you to speak with clarity and confidence about your students' progress.

Truly valuable assessment is based on clearly articulated goals, and is ongoing, rhythmic, and composed of types of tasks that are familiar to students. Ongoing assessment reveals progress over time, so a teacher can compare one assessment to another and "read" growth.

Plan for assessment as you plan instruction. When you ask yourself, "What do my students need to know?" and, "How will they learn it?" don't forget to include, "How will they demonstrate what they've learned?"

The types of assessment you use in each curriculum area will depend on your school's requirements, your values as a teacher, and your personal style. Assessment may be built into a project or be treated as a stand-alone activity. Sources for assessment can include reviews that come with published curriculum materials, teacher-created assessment activities, student goal-setting and self-evaluation, teacher observations and anecdotal notes, and formal or informal standardized tests.

However you manage assessment, building it into your calendar is the key to staying on top of it. Therefore, I suggest you create an Assessment Schedule (see sample on page 113) and integrate it into the Working Calendar. Use a copy of the schedule template on page 124 to determine the types of formal and informal assessments you'll use and how often you'll need to make each assessment. Then add the dates for these assessments to your Working Calendar (see Step 2 under Six Steps to Creating a Working Calendar on page 23). Taking this step assures you that you will remain generally aware of your students' progress across the curriculum. Of course, if the need for additional assessments arises unexpectedly or certain kinds of assessments are not needed as frequently as you had expected, you can always change the schedule.

Remember that the Assessment Schedule form is for planning purposes only; once you establish a schedule as shown in the sample below, incorporate the dates into your Working Calendar.

ASSESSMENT SCHEDULE
(This form is for planning only; incorporate dates into your Working Calendar.)

Curriculum Area	Components/Modes of Assessment	Assessment Pattern/Dates
Reading	Running Records	October, January, March, and May
	Update independent reading list	First Monday of the month
Math	Current focus	Reflection Journal (occasional)
	Skills maintenance	Homework (daily); quizzes (every other Friday)
Writing	Writing conferences	Ongoing, weekly or biweekly (rotate through class in alphabetical order, each week if large class)
	Published projects	End of unit

RESOURCE PAGES

Reflection Journals

I developed Reflection Journals in collaboration with a colleague, Jennifer Haakmat, when we were both fourth-grade teachers in Brooklyn. We needed an assessment tool that would give us an idea of how individual students—and the class as a whole—were integrating and applying new concepts across the curriculum. Besides informing our planning, the journals were very useful tools in preparing for parent conferences.

Here are some examples of Reflection Journal assignments in several curriculum areas.

Social Studies

In our discussions about immigration, we've talked a lot about the idea of "culture," and the way in which immigrants have to adapt to their new home. Think for a minute about our **classroom culture**. What do we **value** in our classroom? How can you tell? Do we have **rituals** that bring us together? What do we **celebrate**? What gives us our **identity**?

> Well I'm thinking that our classroom has a kind of culture. When we first started in September I didn't know what it was. But it's kind of like I immigrated from third grade.
> We value writing a lot. We wrote memoirs and now we're working on poetry and everyone's really proud of the poetry. We also value listening to each other. We also value taking care of our room and the plants. We also value other 4th graders

Science

My sister and I disagreed about whether gloves or mittens are warmer in the winter. To settle our disagreement, we decided to do an experiment: We got out a pair of wool mittens and a pair of insulated nylon gloves. Each of us put on one mitten and one glove and went out to play in the snow. After half an hour, we came back in and talked about which hand felt warmer—the one with the mitten, or the one with the glove. We both felt the gloved hand was warmer, so we decided that gloves are warmer than mittens.

Was our experiment fair? If you think it wasn't fair, explain what we would need to change in order to make it fair.

> **Experiment**
>
> I think that the experiment was not fair. I think that, because the mittens were made from wool and the gloves were made out of nylon. I think they should have used the same mitirial for both mittans and gloves. Then they go outside and play in the snow for a half an hour. Then they will wich one is hotter. This is what I think about this experiment.

> **!** If you have journals or writer's notebooks to review on a weekly basis but have trouble getting through the whole stack in a single sitting, consider dividing the whole class into three, four, or five groups and assigning each group a review day. Leafing through five or six notebooks each day during lunch breaks or preps will make the task less daunting—and, most likely, keep you from getting exhausted and distracted.

Spelling

Look at the word pairs below:

evacuate / evacuation

accuse / accusation

apply / application

create / creation

Do you notice any spelling changes? What are they? Do you notice any meaning changes? Using one word pair as an example, explain the meaning change or write a sentence for each word in the pair.

> Word pairs:
> 1A. Evacuate 1B. Evacuatation
> 2A. Accuse   2B. Accusation
> 3A. Apply   3B. Application
> 4A. Create   4B. Creation
>
> 1. I noticed some spelling changes of the groups of words A and B. Take the word evacuate for example, the last letter is e and then in group B it is changed to evacutation, with -ation added.

Tips for Using Reflection Journals Successfully

Set aside one or two brief writing periods weekly (usually 15–20 minutes each) for writing in the journals. Formulate assignments that will give you a clear idea of how well your students understand pivotal concepts in your curriculum. When giving instructions for completing the assignments, ask students not only to explain what they understand, but also to ask questions or describe what was still unclear to them. Accept thoughtful and thorough explanations presented as narratives, lists, organized notes, charts, drawings, and so forth.

Record-Keeping and Reporting Student Progress

When your goals are clear (see Chapter 2) and you have mechanisms in place for tracking everyone's progress, reporting that progress is a straightforward process. You can state with confidence what your goals are and where they come from, how your curriculum addresses them, how your students are progressing toward them, and what the obstacles appear to be.

All teachers need to create a record-keeping system to track students' progress toward goals in every curriculum area. Depending on the modes of assessment you plan to use, you will need to develop a personalized method of record-keeping parallel to—but separate from—the actual work that children produce. For practical reasons, teachers need to make notes in an informal, unedited, and shorthand way. These notes are only shared with students and parents at the discretion of the teacher, and therefore should be kept entirely separate from student work. Label any binder containing assessments or related notes "Confidential" and keep it out of sight when either students or their parents are in the room.

Your record-keeping tools will serve you best if they're simple, portable, and accessible. I recommend using a single three-inch-thick binder with a section devoted to each student. Each student's section may contain:

- formal assessments, checklists, or graphs such as those pertaining to guided reading

- anecdotal notes about academics or social issues

- copies of student work that may be particularly useful in illustrating your point in a parent conference

- a list of any goals you have set for (or with) the student

> **!** Remember to keep all records up to date by sticking to the assessment schedule you've added to your Working Calendar.

- notes from conferences or phone conversations with parents, tutors, therapists, and so on
- substantive notes or e-mails from parents, colleagues, or administrators regarding the student

In addition, it's helpful to keep a copy of the report card or form in your binder, to focus your assessment.

Using Records Effectively

The time and effort you put into designing a record-keeping system at the beginning of the year will pay off tremendously when it's time for parent conferences and report writing. Most important, you will not have to begin assessing your students just for the occasion: The process will have been ongoing since the opening of school (see Truly Useful Assessment, pages 112–113). In addition to providing you with a more professional presentation at parent conferences, ongoing assessment will guide and inform your teaching.

The way in which your records support the process of report writing will vary widely depending on the kind of report you use. However, if you have maintained good records, you are prepared for a whole range of possibilities. You will be able to write detailed narrative reports based on your students' level of achievement in relation to established standards, and you will, if asked, be able to articulate the reasoning behind the choice of a checkmark category like "meets standard" or "unsatisfactory," or even a letter grade.

Whether parent conferences precede, follow, or coincide with written reports, the two modes of reporting should be consistent and aligned in content. Truthfully, this guideline only makes things easier: Use report writing as a way to prepare for parent conferences, or parent conferences as a way to prepare for report writing. Either way, the sources of your comments—the ongoing assessment system you have developed—remain the same.

! **There are some things that may be appropriate to discuss in parent conferences but *not* to put into writing. These guidelines vary from school to school, but in general, recommendations for tutoring, therapy, or psycho-educational evaluation are not mentioned in a printed report. If you feel such a recommendation should be included, be sure you have first cleared the decision with an administrator.**

The qualities of good conferring apply to good report writing as well:

- Begin, if the report form allows it, with what the child does well.
- Be specific and provide examples if you can.
- Only say what you know.
- Avoid jargon.

Guidelines for Conducting Successful Parent Conferences

In most cases, meetings with parents are cordial, productive, informative, and useful to both educators and parents. However, some conferences do go awry. Sometimes parents behave badly. In addition, when teachers fail to listen to parents, are vague in their assessments, or are unprepared to address issues that are important to parents, the meetings can be tense, even volatile, and of little use to anyone. If you keep the following guidelines in mind, you may avoid the most common pitfalls.

1. **Do some research first.** I send home a notice a couple of weeks before parent conferences, asking parents what their main concerns and questions are. I staple their responses directly to my conference notes, in order to guide my own preparation (see the reproducible Sample Letter on page 125).

2. **Use your established assessment system.** Don't start from scratch—most of your work is already done! Review any checklists or notes you've been using for ongoing assessment. Decide whether to have the checklist with you at the conference or use it to create a conference note form (see next item). The checklist may be unnecessarily specific for the conference, or you may not want parents to see your raw notes. If either of these is the case (and this is quite likely), use a simplified form as described in number 3, below.

Take good notes and put them where you'll see them!

You have a responsibility to learn from parent conferences. Conversations with parents often will provide you with new insights and help you clarify goals for your students. If your notes involve some kind of follow-up—for example, finding the name of a tutor, making a referral to the learning specialist, or scheduling an extra meeting—add them directly to your Planbook (I use sticky notes for this purpose), so you're sure to see it again within a day.

3. **Organize your notes into simple categories on a conference note form.** Include only the most vital and relevant standards in each curriculum area, and the simplest and most useful of rating categories—for example, Areas of Strength, Areas of Concern, and Goals. Using a grid or following a simple conference note form allows you to notice quickly whether your presentation will give the overall picture you want to convey. For example, will you sound more negative than you intend to? Do you need to find more to add to the "strengths" category? (See the reproducible Parent Conference Form on page 126).

4. **Ask your students how they think they're doing.** Although as the teacher you have a broad and sophisticated perspective on student progress, asking students to reflect on their own work can be very useful. They are very likely to provide additional insights into areas of growth or challenge, or draw your attention to something you've missed.

5. **Be prepared with samples of student work.** Parents should leave a conference with a clear idea as well as concrete examples of what's going well, and what areas need work. While it's not a good idea to overwhelm parents with a whole semester's worth of written work, well-chosen samples will support and clarify your salient points. (See page 103 for ideas.)

6. ***Always* begin with what the child does well.** Without exception, human beings are more receptive to constructive criticism—even bad news—when our hard work, honest attempts, and natural talents are noticed and remarked upon. Parents identify with their children and, in many cases, experienced similar academic or social circumstances themselves when they were young. It's vitally important to them that you see their children as individuals and that you like them. In some cases, you may have to search high and low for a success story. It's worth it if you want to be heard when you recommend an evaluation, a change in reading group, or a tutor.

7. **Only say what you know.** Don't feel you have to report on every area of the curriculum. Get an idea of what each family's priorities are (you can do this by sending home that form before conference time), and discuss what seems most relevant. It's perfectly acceptable to say, "I need to do a little research on that, and I'll get back to you" if a parent asks you something you are not prepared to answer. This response, if stated confidently and unapologetically, is perfectly professional, and certainly is preferable to making something up on the spot.

    If a parent is disrespectful or unpleasant ("What's with the homework? It's for babies!"), don't feel you have to defend yourself. Maintain your composure by acknowledging the comment without engaging with the parent unnecessarily: "Hmm. You find the homework too easy. I'll make note of that. Can you give me a brief example of what you mean?" Write the feedback on your notes, and then *immediately* regain control of the conference by returning to *your* agenda, and your prepared materials.

8. **Avoid jargon.** Using overwrought professional vocabulary or this month's educational buzzword actually makes your dialogue with parents less substantial. Instead of using catchphrases or technical terms, describe what you mean or demonstrate it with examples or concrete materials. For instance, instead of using the term *miscue* when discussing a student's reading, try, "When reading aloud, Irene frequently substitutes one word for another, similar-looking word. For example, on this page, she read 'understandable' instead of 'unmanageable.'" Make your written reports concise and jargon-free as well.

9. **Show that you know the child by having an anecdote ready to share.** As described in number 6 above, parents deeply appreciate your knowledge of their child, above and beyond the child's academic abilities. A brief story about a comment made in a class meeting, a journal entry, or a social interaction can personalize a conference and make it more satisfying for parents. Recently, I met with a mother whose daughter, Amy, had long struggled with numerous academic difficulties. This mother was, understandably, particularly anxious—and wary that her child's daily trips to the resource room made her a social outsider. This was not the case, and in order to convince her mother of that fact, I described an incident during which Amy successfully mediated a conflict between two of her classmates. The anecdote provided a snapshot of Amy's social life, and it also reassured Amy's mother that I recognized her daughter's wisdom and valued her presence in my class.

10. **Anticipate frequently asked questions.** If you are new to teaching, to a school, or to a grade level, consult more experienced teachers to find out what parents typically ask about. Frequently, parents at particular grade levels may be preoccupied with testing, progress in reading, the transition to middle school, and other matters. While you don't want these concerns to overwhelm your agenda, you should be prepared to respond to them.

Summary

Personalize and refine the suggestions in this chapter until they suit your style and teaching environment. The materials and methods described here are one example of a functional, successful system—but many more versions are possible. When making changes to the suggestions here, use the following list of priorities as a guide.

- Begin by preventing clutter whenever (and wherever) possible.

- Mentally follow the path of a student assignment from beginning to end—through corrections, revisions, completion, sharing or display, and being archived or sent home. Looking at the process from both your point of view and your students', minimize opportunities for student work to get lost or remain unfinished.

- Create regular space in your schedule, such as Worktime (see page 107), during which slower workers can catch up and faster workers can find new challenges.

- Process homework assignments in the same way as classwork assignments, and hold them to the same standard.

- Plan for and schedule assessment as you plan instruction, and incorporate assessment into your work every day.

Your organizational system will be most efficient if it's integrated with the tools described in Chapter 2. When you plan assessment, add it to the Calendar Pages of your Working Calendar. If your class lists for recent weeks reveal that many students are behind schedule on a project, make notes on the Monthly Focus Pages and adjust your planning when necessary (see Chapter 2 Summary for suggestions). When you jot down reminders to follow up on a meeting with a parent, do so in your Planbook. As you and your students choose work to archive or send home, photocopy representative samples and add them to Artifact Binders. Your goal is to keep things simple for yourself and your students, and to plan more successfully with each passing year.

ASSESSMENT SCHEDULE

(This form is for planning only; incorporate dates into your Working Calendar.)

Curriculum Area	Components/Modes of Assessment	Assessment Pattern/Dates

PREPARING FOR CONFERENCES *Sample Letter*

Dear _____,

   I look forward to meeting with you on _____ to discuss _____'s progress in school. As you know, our conference time is limited. In an effort to make conferences as focused, productive, and satisfying as possible, I'm asking all parents to identify in advance those issues that are of greatest interest or concern to them. This will allow me to take your priorities into account as I plan each conference. Please take a few minutes to share your thoughts in the space below. Kindly return the bottom portion of this form by _____.

                                        Thank you,

- -

Student's name: _____

Parent(s) or guardian(s) completing this form: _____

Who will be attending the conference? _____

The areas I/we are most interested in discussing include:

Additional comments or questions:

PARENT CONFERENCE FORM

Student's name _____ Date of conference: _____

Present at conference: _____

Parent interests/concerns expressed in advance of conference

Areas of Strength (attach representative work samples)

Areas of Concern (attach representative work samples)

Goals and Plans for Support

Recommendations made at the conference for support services, enrichment, or further inquiry

Teacher/administrative follow-up/additional meetings (include dates, if appropriate)

Conclusion

One of the great joys of teaching is the chance to start fresh every year. The ideas in *Your Best Year Yet!* are intended to help you take advantage of that opportunity.

As you work your way through each school year, you will undoubtedly encounter obstacles: glitches in your systems, wrenches in your plans. The relentless pace of school will probably require that you patch things up as best you can, and sometimes that will mean designing short-term solutions to complex problems. Reality may dictate that you have to let go of some of your goals for the time being. When that happens, use the tools in this book to widen your perspective and prepare for the following year. For example:

- Cultivate and invigorate a sense of community in your classroom. Add your own ideas to those in this book.

- Make notes in your Working Calendar when a project seems too ambitious or too limited for the time you allotted to it.

- Create or personalize forms for your Planbook to address an organizational need that has become a chronic annoyance.

- Eliminate clutter whenever you can, especially at the end of the year, using Clearing Out and Paring Down strategies (Chapter 3).

- Continually add ideas to your Early Days and Weeks plans (Chapter 2) and Extension binders (Chapter 4) as the year progresses; even if you don't get to them this year, you can develop them next year.

Teaching is immensely satisfying, despite the fact that no matter how hard you work, you may never feel quite finished. When you love your work, you will always have a mind full of ideas and possibilities. I hope the ideas in *Your Best Year Yet!* will help you realize more and more of those possibilities as the years go on.

Index

A

archived work, 99–103
  binders, portfolios for, 101–102
  personalizing, organizing, 102
  sending home, 103
Artifact Binders, 19, 49–50
  keeping, current, 51
assessments, 112–113
assignments, reviewing, returning, 106–107

C

class lists, 105
classroom community, 9
  See also community building principles
classroom design
  eliminating clutter, creating storage, 78–79
  grid, 77
  guiding questions for, 75–76
  refinement, 76
classroom design examples
  cozy "Quiet Area," 73
  group clusters, 68–69
  "one-room schoolhouse" style, 70
  small-group work with tables, 74
  whole-group experience, 71
classroom design principles, 63–66
  arrangement, values and expectations and, 63
  excess, letting go of, 66
  learning context variations and, 64
  opportunities for change and, 66
  structure, flexibility and, 65
  students sense of ownership and, 65
classroom maintenance
  jobs, 92
  student allies and, 89–90
clutter. *See* paper management
community building principles, 9–15
  accomplishment celebration, 14
  expectations, skills and, 14
  good listening, modeling, 9
  inclusion, tolerance, 12
  making all students stars, 10
  schoolwork context variation, 11
  social, emotional development, 10
  student responsibility, leadership, 11
conferences, parent, 119–122
containers, 86–87
  shelf space and, 87
current work, 99
curriculum-building resources, 31–44
  guiding questions, 32–35
  school year, shape of, 37–41
  skills, tools approach, 42–44
  standards, using, 36
curriculum planning, 17–61

E

Extensions pockets, 100

H

homework, 107–111
  habits, tracking, 110–111
  notebooks, 107–111

leadership roles, 91–92

M

mailboxes, 111
maintenance. *See* classroom maintenance
materials
  container ideas for, 87
  kits, 88
  placement of, 86–88
  See also organization

N

notebooks, homework, 107–111

O

organization
  assessing storage situation and, 85
  classroom materials and, 80
  materials placement and, 86–88
  sorting materials and, 82–84
  storage and, 81

P

paper management
  archived work and, 99–103
  beginning, ending work periods and, 104
  class lists, current work folders and, 105
  current work and, 99
  guiding questions about, 97
  homework notebooks and, 107–111
  paper clutter and, 95–96
  reviewing, returning assignments and, 106–107
  systems, 98
parent conferences, 119–122
peer support, 91–92
Planbooks, 19, 45–48
  daily balancing, 48
  long-term goals, real time and, 46
  weekly planning, 47
planning
  borrowing, bartering time and, 52
  expectations and, 52
  schedules, rethinking, 52
  time frames, 52
  See also Planbooks; Working Calendars
progress reports. *See* student progress

R

record keeping, 117–119
  effective use of records and, 118–119
Reflection journals, 114–116
room design. *See* classroom design

S

shelf space, limited, 87
storage
  assessing, 85
  container ideas, 87
  creating, 78–79
  material kits, 88
  shelf space alternatives, 87
  types of, 81
student progress
  parent conferences and, 119–122
  record keeping and, 117–119
students
  classroom jobs for, 91–93
  classroom maintenance and, 89–90, 92
  greater school community and, 93
  leadership responsibilities for, 11
  making all stars, 10
  room maintenance jobs for, 92
  social, emotional health of, 10

T

teacher's helpers, 91

W

work folders, class lists and, 105
Working Calendars, 18, 20–30
  adding basic information to, 23
  assembling, 20, 30
  Calendar Page, 20, 54
  gathering materials for, 22–23
  goal sequencing for, 26
  Monthly Focus Page, 21, 27–29, 56
  Planbooks and, 46
  projects, activities and, 28–29
  strategies, skills, tools and, 28
  themes, connections and, 29
  Year-Long Goals Form and, 24–26, 55